NUGGETS of TRUTH from GOD'S WORD

A Compilation of Teachings from The River at Tampa Bay

Rodney and Adonica Howard-Browne

RMI Publications
P. O. Box 292888
Tampa, FL • 33687 • USA

NUGGETS *of* TRUTH *from* GOD'S WORD

ISBN 1-884662-11-0
Copyright © 1998 by Revival Ministries International
Printed in the United States of America

Published by RMI Publications
P. O. Box 292888 • Tampa FL • 33687 • USA
Phone: 813-971-9999
Fax: 813-971-0701
www.revival.com

All rights reserved under International Copyright Law. No part of this publication may be reproduced, stored in a retrieval system, or transmitted, in whole or in part, in any form or by any means, electronic, mechanical, photocopying, recording, or otherwise, without the prior express consent of the publisher.

Unless otherwise indicated, all scriptural references are from *The King James Version* of the Bible.

Selected scriptures are taken from *The Amplified Bible*, copyright ©1987 by The Zondervan Corporation.

NUGGETS *of* TRUTH *from* GOD'S WORD

Table of Contents

		Page No.
Foreword		5
Chapter 1	Overcoming Fear	6
Chapter 2	Having a Godly Marriage	8
Chapter 3	Why Some Fall Under the Power	11
Chapter 4	For Unto Us a Son is Born	13
Chapter 5	What Does the Future Hold?	15
Chapter 6	To You, In You, and Through You	17
Chapter 7	God's Life-Giving Word	20
Chapter 8	The Touch of the Master's Hand	23
Chapter 9	Don't Put God in a Box	25
Chapter 10	Faithful to Forgive	27
Chapter 11	Stay Hungry and Thirsty for God	31
Chapter 12	Being a Doer of the Word	33
Chapter 13	The Cause of Revival	35
Chapter 14	Standing in the Storms of Life	37
Chapter 15	Breaking the Curse of Poverty	39
Chapter 16	Watch Your Mouth and Say What the Bible Says About you	41
Chapter 17	Live Long — Live Healthy — Do It God's Way	45
Chapter 18	A Revival Greater Than Pentecost	48
Chapter 19	The Joy of Our Salvation	51
Chapter 20	Seven Redemptive Names of God	54
Chapter 21	A Sign Spoken Against	57
Chapter 22	The Suddenlies of God	60
Chapter 23	As a Man Thinks, So is He	62
Chapter 24	A Speck and A Beam	64
Chapter 25	The Land of the Free and the Home of the Brave	66
Chapter 26	Summer Campmeeting — A History	69
Chapter 27	Rightly Dividing the Word of Truth	71
Chapter 28	No Private Interpretation of God's Word	74
Chapter 29	Remembering the Onions	76
Chapter 30	Fighting the Zuzims and Zamzummims of Life	79
Chapter 31	I Am That I Am	82
Chapter 32	Our Christian Code of Conduct	84
Chapter 33	Agreement — The Key to Answered Prayer and A Successful Life	87

Table of Contents - continued   Page No.

Chapter 34	Spiritual Hunger	90
Chapter 35	Being Faithful with That with Which the Lord Has Blessed You	92
Chapter 36	Giving as a Lifestyle	94
Chapter 37	How to Give According to the Word of God	96
Chapter 38	The Glory of God	98
Chapter 39	The Pure in Heart Shall Prosper	101
Chapter 40	The Restorer of Wasted Years	103
Chapter 41	The Communion of the Blood and Body of Christ	105
Chapter 42	Methods and the Anointing	107
Chapter 43	The Power of Forgiveness	110
Chapter 44	Healing—Is it God's Will?	113
Chapter 45	Faith's Definitions	116
Chapter 46	Tithes and Offerings	119
Chapter 47	The Lord is Building the House	122
Chapter 48	The Blessing of the Lord	124
Chapter 49	Glad Tidings of Great Joy	127
Chapter 50	All These Things Did Jesus Do	130
Chapter 51	King of Kings and Lord of Lords	132
Chapter 52	The Power in Your Words	135
Chapter 53	Different Kinds of Prayer	137
Chapter 54	Delight and Desire	141
Chapter 55	All-Night Prayer—Praying Unto God	143
Chapter 56	Breaking the Mold of Religious Tradition	145
Chapter 57	Free at Last	148
Chapter 58	No More Judgment	151
Chapter 59	Faith—The Title Deed	154
Chapter 60	Believing God for Big Things	157
Chapter 61	Do Not Be the Judge	160
Chapter 62	Be Your Own Judge	163
Chapter 63	God's Word is True and Sure	166
Chapter 64	Train Your Child While There is Hope	169
Chapter 65	Our Deliverer Has Come	171
Chapter 66	A Spirit of Wisdom and Revelation	174
Chapter 67	Partnership	176

FOREWORD

We trust this book will be a blessing to you. When we started The River at Tampa Bay, the Lord instructed us to put a teaching in our weekly bulletin for our congregation. This teaching letter was to cover many different subjects that would be a blessing to the congregation and guide, encourage, admonish, and inspire them. This has been our way of sharing truths that have changed our lives.

This book is a compilation of the teachings we have published thus far. We trust that as you prayerfully read them, the Lord will speak to your heart and bless you as much as we were blessed when we put them to paper.

Thank you, Carol Patterson, for your diligence and hard work in putting *Nuggets of Truth* together.

> Dr. Rodney and Adonica Howard-Browne
> The River at Tampa Bay
> Tampa, Florida
> June, 1998

ONE
OVERCOMING FEAR

II Timothy 1:7 (Amp) *For God did not give us a spirit of timidity (of cowardice, of craven and cringing and fawning fear), but [He has given us a spirit] of power and of love and of calm and well-balanced mind and discipline and self-control.*

This scripture has been quoted over the years in regard to victory over fear. Let us look at verse 6, because in the context of the chapter, verse 6 adds light to verse 7.

Vs. 6 *That is why I would remind you to stir up (rekindle the embers of, fan the flame of, and keep burning) the [gracious] gift of God, [the inner fire] that is in you by means of the laying on of my hands [with those of the elders at your ordination].*

This scripture tells us to stir up the gift that was given to us. Because of fear, many people have backed away from what God has called them to do.

The Bible teaches us in **Proverbs 29:25** that *"the fear of man bringeth a snare."* Many are afraid of what other people have to say about them. The truth is that God has a plan for your life and He has given you gifts and talents. However, you have an enemy of your faith that will try to stop the plan of God for your life. This enemy is called *fear*. It will paralyze you and hold you captive. Fear takes many forms: fear of the unknown, fear of failure, fear of success, and many others. Fears can dominate your life until you are so controlled by them that they distort your personality. Are you insecure about your marriage? Do you distrust your partner? Are you constantly worried about the future? About money? About your job?

Do not fear! God is on your side and He will bring you through even the worst conditions in your life. He will never fail you or let you down. Cast your fears on Him today, stir up the gift that is in you, and be blessed. You can be more of a blessing to others when you are operating out of faith rather than fear.

You can be proactive in life rather than reactive. Proactive people operate in faith, doing what God wants them to do. They conduct their lives in a way that accomplishes much for God. Reactive people react to every problem and live in a defense mode. They make decisions based on their fears and insecurities, instead of on their faith in God's ability to see them through. **Romans 14:23b** . . . *for whatsoever is not of faith is sin.*

Stir up the gift, get bold, and walk in faith. Today is your day for victory over fear!

TWO
HAVING A GODLY MARRIAGE

Ephesians 5:22-33 (Amp) Vs. 22 *Wives, be subject (be submissive and adapt yourselves) to your own husbands as [a service] to the Lord.* Vs. 23 *For the husband is head of the wife as Christ is the Head of the church, Himself the Savior of [His] body.* Vs. 24 *As the church is subject to Christ, so let wives also be subject in everything to their husbands.*

Vs. 25 *Husbands, love your wives, as Christ loved the church and gave Himself up for her.* Vs. 26 *So that He might sanctify her, having cleansed her by the washing of water with the Word,* Vs. 27 *That He might present the church to Himself in glorious splendor, without spot or wrinkle or any such things [that she might be holy and faultless].*

Vs. 28 *Even so husbands should love their wives as [being in a sense] their own bodies. He who loves his own wife loves himself.* Vs. 29 *For no man ever hated his own flesh, but nourishes and carefully protects and cherishes it, as Christ does the church,* Vs. 30 *Because we are members (parts) of His body.*

Vs. 31 *For this reason a man shall leave his father and his mother and shall be joined to his wife, and the two shall become one flesh.* Vs. 32 *This mystery is very great, but I speak concerning [the relation of] Christ and the church.* Vs. 33 *However, let each man of you [without exception] love his wife as [being in a sense] his very own self; and let the wife see that she respects and reverences her husband [that she notices him, regards him, honors him, prefers him, venerates, and esteems him; and that she defers to him, praises him, and loves and admires him exceedingly].*

Verse 22 says, *Wives, be subject to your husbands as a **service to the Lord**.* A godly marriage must have God's Word as the foundation of the relationship. God's Word is the handbook for successful, godly marriages that last a lifetime and bring glory to God.

As far as some men are concerned, God placed women on earth for their benefit alone. Their attitude is, "When I say jump, JUMP!" That is not how God intended it to be. He intended for one man and one woman to come together as one flesh. As they grow together, the husband takes the headship according to verse 23, and *then* the wife becomes subject to her husband in everything. This is not something that can be demanded, but actually comes forth when verse 25 is practiced: *Husbands, love your wives.*

A wife can easily submit to her husband as he loves her as Christ loved the church and gave Himself for the church. That agape love — self sacrificial love that does not consider its own needs but the needs of others — is the love these scriptures talk about.

Verse 28 says . . . *leave your father and mother* . . . Too many marriages have broken up because of family ties and domination, or interference by either parent toward the husband or wife. It is important that the husband and wife be in unity, inseparable without any outside influences.

If you want to get into trouble with me, try interfering in my marriage or "laying down the law" to my wife. Things will not be well with you. Adonica and I decided that no one, including our respective parents, would divide us or come between us. No outside force or influence would be allowed to bring strife. One will put a thousand to flight and two will put ten thousand to flight—two are better than one!

Communication is one of the greatest keys in maintaining a healthy, godly marriage. You must spend many hours talking things through, from how many children to have, to child discipline, money matters, and the many other issues affecting your life together.

A good marriage requires a lot of time and effort. Adjust and repair, stay flexible, always be willing to change, and keep your heart soft and tender. Do not let the sun go down on your wrath, even if it means staying up until three o'clock in the morning to get things straightened out.

Finally, do not invest all your time in your kids or you will find yourself living with a spouse you don't know when the children leave the home. Many people divorce after a number of years because they can't live with each other alone. Their lives were spent investing in their children and they find that they have grown apart through the years. Make a decision to base your marriage on God's Word and learn to forgive quickly. In a day and age when marriages are breaking up on every side, you can make it with the help of the Holy Ghost. He'll make the difference!

THREE
WHY SOME FALL UNDER *the* POWER

Recently I was stopped by a member of our congregation and asked for the scriptural references to the question of why some fall under the power of the Holy Spirit.

"Fall under the power" is a better term than "slain in the Spirit," a term widely used in Pentecostal and charismatic circles today. Ananias and Sapphira were "slain in the Spirit." Wouldn't you really rather fall under the power?

Q. Is this scriptural and why?

A. Yes, it is scriptural. There are scriptural references from Genesis to Revelation which I will list for you below.

Q. Why do people fall?

A. It is very simple — when the natural comes in contact with the supernatural, something has to give way, and it's going to be the natural.

SCRIPTURE REFERENCES

1. Genesis 17:1-3 When God appears to Abram, he falls flat on his face (and God talks with him). I believe God can speak to people when they are out under the power. (Now remember, this is not the *only* way, but one of the methods He uses to get our attention.)

2. I Kings 8:10, 11; II Chronicles 5:13, 14 The priests

could not stand to minister because of the cloud. The cloud of God's presence overwhelmed them.

II Chronicles 7:1-3 The priests could not enter into the house of the Lord because of the glory. Let's look at other scriptures where this occurred, when people trembled and shook under God's power.

Habakkuk 3:1-4 *His brightness was as the light* (spoken of the Lord). He had bright beams coming from His hand—if He touched you, you would know it.

3. John 18:1-6 When a band of men and officers from the chief priests and elders came to capture Jesus, He said to them, "Whom do you seek?" And they said, "Jesus of Nazareth." As soon as He said, "I am He," they fell to the ground.

4. The Apostle Paul (formerly Saul of Tarsus) fell to the ground under the power and was born again. (Acts 9:1-4; Acts 22:6-8)

5. Peter fell into a trance and saw a vision. (Acts 10:10)

6. On the Isle of Patmos when John saw Jesus, he fell at His feet as dead. (Revelation 1:12-17)

Falling under the power is a supernatural manifestation of the Spirit of God. When you are on the floor, God can speak to you. We call it "lying on God's operating table." Don't resist the Spirit of God; He'll never hurt you. Yield to Him, rest in His presence, and He will touch you in a special way. I pray that you will study these scriptures personally and cross-reference them to see what else God's Word has to say about His display of His glory in the church.

FOUR
FOR UNTO *us* A SON *is* BORN

Isaiah 7:14 (Amp) *Therefore the Lord Himself shall give you a sign: Behold, the young woman who is unmarried and a virgin shall conceive and bear a son, and shall call his name Immanuel [God with us].*

Luke 2:10, 11 (Amp) *But the angel said to them, Do not be afraid; for behold, I bring you good news of a great joy which will come to all the people. For to you is born this day in the town of David a Savior, Who is Christ (the Messiah) the Lord!*

I John 3:8 (Amp) *[But] he who commits sin [who practices evildoing] is of the devil [takes his character from the evil one], for the devil has sinned (violated the divine law) from the beginning. The reason the Son of God was made manifest (visible) was to undo (destroy, loosen, and dissolve) the works the devil [has done].*

It is an historical fact that Jesus was born. Scholars dispute whether He was all God or all man or part God or part man, but we know, from the Bible, that He was God manifest in the flesh. He is completely God and completely man.

Think about this: His birth, death and resurrection have affected the earth like none other before or since. He was the Word made flesh and dwelt among us. He affected the timetable of a whole planet—this is not something you can deny or ignore.

Isaiah 9:6 (Amp) *For to us a Child is born, to us a Son is given;*

and the government shall be upon His shoulder, and His name shall be called Wonderful Counselor, Mighty God, Everlasting Father [of Eternity], Prince of Peace.

His name shall be called "Wonderful" because He is so wonderful; there is none like Him in all the earth. Our Lord Jesus Christ is wonderful in His saving, healing and delivering power. Wonderful in His miraculous virgin birth, wonderful in His sinless life, wonderful in His miracle ministry of signs and wonders. Wonderful in His conquest of sin, sickness, and Satan at Calvary. Wonderful in His supernatural resurrection from the dead. Wonderful in His present-day ministry interceding for us at the Father's right hand in heaven. Wonderful in His power to cleanse and forgive every sin. Wonderful in His ability to free every captive. Wonderful in His grace that heals the brokenhearted and breaks every bondage. He is wonderful because His love reaches out to touch and transform all who will come to Him and call upon His Name.

Acts 4:12 (Amp) *And there is salvation in and through no one else, for there is no other name under heaven given among men by and in which we must be saved. Reflect again on the goodness of God. As Christians, we have something to shout about and celebrate, because Jesus lives, and in Him we live and move and have our being.*

FIVE
WHAT DOES *the* FUTURE HOLD?

James 4:13, 14 (Amp) Vs. 13 *Come now, you who say, Today or tomorrow we will go into such and such a city and spend a year there and carry on our business and make money.*

Vs. 14 *Yet you do not know [the least thing] about what may happen tomorrow. What is the nature of your life? You are [really] but a wisp of vapor (a puff of smoke, a mist) that is visible for a little while and then disappears [into thin air].*

What does the future hold? If this question has not been on our lips, it has been in our thoughts. In a couple of years we will close out a decade, a century and a millennium! Into the twenty-first century we go, for some a frightening prospect. But as Christians we don't fear the future because we know Who holds the future—His Name is JESUS!

There was a very popular song during the '70s and '80s entitled "He's Got the Whole World in His Hands." We can know that He has us in the palm of His Hand. He is with us, will never leave us nor forsake us, and He is a friend Who sticks closer than a brother. The Bible says that in the last days men's hearts will fail them for fear of the things that are coming. Aren't you excited that you and I can have peace no matter what? God must have felt that you had what it takes to live in this day and hour because He allowed you to be in the Kingdom for such a time as this. You have been made out of the right kind of stuff. You are just like Shadrach, Meshach and Abednego—even though you go through the fire, it will not burn you. Even though the circumstances look bleak, if you trust Him, He will bring you through.

As the Body of Christ, we need to know that we do not consult psychics (the devil) regarding our future. We have God's Word and His Holy Spirit to lead and guide us. He will show us what we need to know about the things to come.

He holds the future and He holds us!

SIX
TO YOU, *in* YOU, *and* THROUGH YOU

The Holy Spirit is the revealer of Jesus to the believer, in the believer, and through the believer.

JESUS REVEALED TO *the* BELIEVER BY *the* HOLY SPIRIT

John 16:14, 15 Vs. 14 *He shall glorify me: for he shall receive of mine, and shall show it unto you.* Vs. 15 *All things that the Father hath are mine: therefore said I, that he shall take of mine, and shall show it unto you.*

No one knows Jesus as well as the Holy Spirit. He was with Christ when they both preexisted with the Father through eternity past. He was with Him throughout His earthly ministry, through the sacrifice of the cross, and the glorious resurrection. The Holy Spirit reveals the nature and character of Jesus to the believer. Through the work of the Holy Spirit, Jesus comes alive to us. He walks out of the pages of the gospels and becomes real and alive in our hearts.

JESUS REVEALED IN *the* BELIEVER BY *the* HOLY GHOST

Galatians 1:15, 16 Vs. 15 *But when it pleased God, who separated me from my mother's womb, and called me by His grace,* Vs. 16 *To reveal his Son in me, that I might preach him among the heathen . . .*

The main purpose of the plan of redemption—Jesus giving His life—was to restore man to the image of God, as he was before the fall of Adam. After you become born again (John 3:3), the Holy Spirit's desire is to place Christ's nature and likeness in your heart (and the heart of every born-again believer) by revealing Christ *in* you.

As the Holy Spirit is allowed to work in your life, you will have the fruit of the Spirit (as mentioned in Galatians 5:22, 23), and you will grow *daily* into the measure of the stature of the fullness of Christ (Ephesians 4:13). We need a *daily* revival in our lives. We need God's *power*, His *nature* and His *glory* revealed *to* us and *in* us so we can show forth His glory, which is His desire for us. This process continues in us until we see Him face to face—growing and changing—becoming more like Him every day.

JESUS REVEALED THROUGH *the* BELIEVER BY *the* HOLY GHOST

Mark 16:20 says the disciples went forth and preached everywhere, and God confirmed the Word with signs following. The Spirit was actually being revealed *through* the believers, as they yielded to the Holy Spirit as willing vessels. Jesus said that the believer would do the works that He did and *greater* works, because He was going to His Father (John 14:12).

Through the believer, the Holy Spirit wants to show the world that Jesus Christ is the same—*yesterday, today, and forever* (Hebrews 13:8). What He did in Bible days He will do today. The Holy Spirit wants to demonstrate the living Lord Jesus through you. He is alive and He is working in the earth today through you and me. My prayer for you is that Christ be formed in you (Galatians 4:19), so you can be all He wants you to be.

Remember:

>**TO** you — the new birth

>**IN** you — which is an ongoing process throughout your Christian walk

>**THROUGH** you — as He demonstrates His power to a lost and dying world

SEVEN
GOD'S *life-giving* WORD

Proverbs 4:20-22 (Amp) Vs. 20 *My son, attend to my words; consent and submit to my sayings.* Vs. 21 *Let them not depart from your sight; keep them in the center of your heart.* Vs. 22 *For they are life to those who find them, healing and health to all their flesh.*

God's Word is life to those who find it and healing and health to all their flesh.

Psalm 107:20 (Amp) *He sends forth His word and heals them and rescues them from the pit and destruction.*

God sent His Word to heal us. The Hebrew word translated "health" in Proverbs is *marpe*, and "heal" in Psalms is *raphah*. However, they mean the same: heal, cure, and make whole. In Proverbs, the word *raphah* also means to mend and repair. We see from the meanings of the Hebrew words that these passages are not referring to *spiritual* healing but to *physical* healing.

Many people go through life accepting second best or, in some cases, *hell on earth*, because they have no idea that there is an answer, a remedy and a cure for their affliction. It does no good to say, "If it is God's will, He will heal me/deliver me." Because then you could also say, "If it is God's will, He will save me." **No!**

If you are a Christian, you should know by now that it is God's will to save you—He sent Jesus long before you were born. In fact, the Bible says that He had **planned** to send

Jesus from the foundation of the world (I Peter 1:20 and Revelation 13:8). Your salvation was planned for you from the foundation of the world, as was your healing and your deliverance.

It is God's will to save us and it is God's will to heal us. How do we know this? We know it because He has told us. How did He tell us? He told us through His Word.

Hebrews 4:3 (Amp) *For we who have believed (adhered to and trusted in and relied on God) do enter that rest, in accordance with His declaration that those [who did not believe] should not enter when He said, As I swore in My wrath, They shall not enter My rest; and this He said although [His] works had been completed and prepared [and waiting for all who would believe] from the foundation of the world.*

God has provided everything we need. All He is waiting for is someone who will believe and in doing so, receive. You see, God's Word is life, health, and healing to us when it becomes real to us—when we believe it!

Psalm 103:5 (Amp) *Who satisfies your mouth [your necessity and desire at your personal age and situation] with good so that your youth, renewed, is like the eagle's [strong, overcoming, soaring]!*

Forgiveness, healing, redemption and provision are all part of the same package as far as God is concerned.

Isaiah 55:10, 11 (Amp) Vs. 10 *For as the rain and snow come down from the heavens, and return not there again, but water the earth and make it bring forth and sprout, that it may give seed to the sower and bread to the eater,* Vs. 11 *So shall My word be that goes forth out of My mouth: it shall not return to Me void [without producing any effect, useless], but it shall accomplish that which I please and purpose, and it shall prosper in the thing for which I sent it.*

God's **will** is His **Word**! Make it part of your life every hour, every day. We must change to agree with God's Word — not change God's Word to suit our opinions and carnal thinking. The Holy Spirit is your teacher, so allow Him to make God's Word and will clear to you. Allow the Word to change you and soon you will begin to see your circumstances change all around you. God will be bringing you into His life and His **health**. His **Word** will work in you and **heal** you.

EIGHT
THE TOUCH of the MASTER'S HAND

Luke 13:11-13 (Amp) Vs. 11 *And there was a woman there who for eighteen years had had an infirmity caused by a spirit (a demon of sickness). She was bent completely forward and utterly unable to straighten herself up or to look upward.* Vs. 12 *And when Jesus saw her, He called [her to Him] and said to her, Woman, you are released from your infirmity!* Vs. 13 *Then He laid [His] hands on her, and instantly she was made straight, and she recognized and thanked and praised God.*

There was something special about the touch of the Lord's hands on this woman and the other people He healed and delivered. **That "something" was the anointing.** When Jesus touches someone's life, **it changes forever!** Jesus can take people who are completely down and out and totally transform them.

No matter what you may be going through—**Jesus cares! He loves you.** He wants to touch and change you. Jesus can take what the world has despised and discarded and rejected and make something beautiful of it. It does not matter what other people think of you. It does not even matter what you think about yourself. If you place your life into His wonderful hands, His miracle-working hands, He can make something beautiful and worthwhile out of what you give Him. He can make something **beautiful** out of **your life.** Here is a poem that has greatly blessed me.

THE TOUCH *of* THE MASTER'S HAND

'Twas battered and scarred,
And the auctioneer thought it scarcely worth his while
    To auction off the old violin,
But he held it up with a smile.
    "What am I bid for the old violin?
Who'll start the bidding for me?
    One dollar. One. Who'll make it two?
Two dollars. Who'll make it three?
Going for three . . ." But no, from a room far back
A gray-haired man came forward and picked up the bow.
    Wiping the dust from the old violin,
And tightening up its strings,
    He played a melody pure and sweet,
As sweet as an angel sings. The auctioneer,
With a voice that was quiet and low,
Said, "What am I bid for the old violin?"
    As he held it up with the bow.
"One thousand, one, who'll make it two?
    Two thousand, who'll make it three?
Three thousand once, three thousand twice,
    Going and gone," said he.
The people cheered, but some of them cried,
    "We don't quite understand
What changed its worth." Quick came the reply,
    "The touch of the master's hand."
Many a man, with life out of tune, battered and torn by sin,
Is auctioned off to a thoughtless crowd,
Much like that old violin. A mess of pottage,
A glass of wine, game, and he travels on.
He's going once, he's going twice,
    He's going . . . he's almost gone.
Then the master comes, and the thoughtless crowd
    Can never quite understand
The worth of a soul and the miracle that's wrought
    By *the touch of the Master's hand.*

                                  Author Unknown

NINE
DON'T *put* GOD *in* A BOX

Isaiah 33:20, 21 (Amp) *Vs. 20 Look upon Zion, the city of our set feasts and solemnities! Your eyes shall see Jerusalem, a quiet habitation, a tent that shall not be taken down; not one of its stakes shall ever be pulled up, neither shall any of its cords be broken. Vs. 21 But there the Lord will be for us in majesty and splendor a place of broad rivers and streams, where no oar-propelled boat can go, and no mighty and stately ship can pass.*

When the Lord spoke to Adonica and me about opening The River at Tampa Bay, He said we were to have a place where He could have free rein, where people could come and worship Him with no manipulation of man.

Verse 21 speaks of a place of broad rivers and streams, where no oar-propelled boat can go. That means nothing propelled by the effort of man is going to go on The River of God. No mighty or stately ship can pass — this means no organization of man can take us where The River of God goes.

Our vision for The River is that we do nothing merely because it's being done elsewhere; we must obey God and do only what He wants done. If we do certain things at The River at Tampa Bay, we will be doing so because we are following the direction of the Holy Spirit.

We thank God for all the churches in the Tampa Bay area, but The River has been raised up by God to fulfill His plan for a revival church for the 21st Century. There are many traveling ministers based at The River and we trust the Lord that many lights will go forth from The River to the far-flung corners of the globe.

Let's make a decision never to put God in a box, because we must allow the Holy Spirit to have free rein at The River. History is waiting to be written; our motto is **to boldly go.** As we go into the 21st Century, the greatest days of revival are upon us.

TEN
FAITHFUL *to* FORGIVE

I John 1:3-6 (Amp) Vs. 3 *What we have seen and [ourselves] heard, we are also telling you, so that you too may realize and enjoy fellowship as partners and partakers with us. And [this] fellowship that we have [which is a distinguishing mark of Christians] is with the Father and with His Son Jesus Christ (the Messiah).* Vs. 4 *And we are now writing these things to you so that our joy [in seeing you included] may be full [and your joy may be complete].*

Vs. 5 *And this is the message [the message of promise] which we have heard from Him and now are reporting to you: God is Light, and there is no darkness in Him at all [no, not in any way].* Vs. 6 *[So] if we say we are partakers together and enjoy fellowship with Him when we live and move and are walking about in darkness, we are [both] speaking falsely and do not live and practice the Truth [which the Gospel presents].*

The Bible says that God is light and if we are in fellowship with Him—then we walk in the light. If we tell people that we are in fellowship with God but we behave as if we are in fellowship with the devil, then we are lying.

I John 1:7 (Amp) *But if we [really] are living and walking in the Light, as He [Himself] is in the Light, we have [true, unbroken] fellowship with one another, and the blood of Jesus Christ His Son cleanses (removes) us from all sin and guilt [keeps us cleansed from sin in all its forms and manifestations].*

How do we walk in the "light"? We walk in the light when we obey God's Word in all we say and do, and when we allow the Holy Ghost to work in our hearts and minds and change us. When we walk in the light, the blood of Jesus cleanses us from guilt and sin and we have true fellowship with our fellow Christians.

I John 1:8-10 (Amp) Vs. 8 *If we say we have no sin [refusing to admit that we are sinners], we delude and lead ourselves astray, and the Truth [which the Gospel presents] is not in us [does not dwell in our hearts].*

Vs. 9 *If we [freely] admit that we have sinned and confess our sins, He is faithful and just (true to His own nature and promises) and will forgive our sins [dismiss our lawlessness] and [continuously] cleanse us from all unrighteousness [everything not in conformity to His will in purpose, thought, and action].*

Vs. 10 *If we say (claim) we have not sinned, we contradict His Word and make Him out to be false and a liar, and His Word is not in us [the divine message of the Gospel is not in our hearts].*

Every person on earth has sinned against God. Sin dwells in your flesh from birth and you are guaranteed to commit sin sometime. As long as we deceive ourselves into believing that we have no sin and have not sinned, God cannot help us with our sin problem. We must admit that sin is wrong and that we have sinned; we must confess our sin to God — and He will instantly forgive us. By the blood of Jesus, God washes away our sins, past, present and future, when we repent of our sins and ask His forgiveness.

While our spirits are born again, our minds and bodies present us with problems — they keep on sinning against God. But if we deal with each problem as it comes up-bring it before the Father, repent and apologize — He will continue to cleanse us and forgive us. Just because God forgave you and washed away your sins when you first received Jesus as your Lord and Savior, does not mean that you are perfectly sinless and will never make a mistake again. If you claim to be sinless, you are a liar, according to verse 10, but when you acknowledge your wrongdoing, God will keep you constantly washed in the blood of Jesus.

I John 2:1, 2 (Amp) Vs. 1 *My little children, I write you these things so that you may not violate God's law and sin. But if anyone should sin, we have an Advocate (One Who will intercede for us) with the Father — [it is] Jesus Christ [the all] righteous [upright, just, Who conforms to the Father's will in every purpose, thought, and action].*

Vs. 2 *And He [that same Jesus Himself] is the propitiation (the atoning sacrifice) for our sins, and not for ours alone but also for [the sins of] the whole world.*

II Corinthians 5:17 (Amp) *Therefore if any person is [ingrafted] in Christ (the Messiah) he is a new creation (a new creature altogether); the old [previous moral and spiritual condition] has passed away. Behold, the fresh and new has come!*

II Corinthians 5:21 (Amp) *For our sake He made Christ [virtually] to be sin Who knew no sin, so that in and through Him we might become [endued with, viewed as being in, and examples of] the righteousness of God [what we ought to be, approved and acceptable and in right relationship with Him, by His goodness].*

Some people have a sin-consciousness. That means they constantly focus on their sin and on the fact that they are unworthy to receive God's forgiveness, even though they may have already repented. The Bible says we have become the righteousness of God — we are in right standing with Him.

We can come boldly into His presence (Hebrews 4:16) to receive mercy and grace, as long as we remember that our righteousness has its source in Jesus. God does not find out about our sin when we confess it; He knows about it when we do it, but He waits for us to humble ourselves, admit our mistakes, and apologize. He is waiting eagerly to forgive us and restore us into fellowship with Him once again, through the blood of His Son, Jesus.

The Father loves us and His desire is for us to walk steadfastly at His side, with unbroken fellowship. If you have sin in your life that has not been confessed and repented of, take care of it right away. Don't spend one more minute out of God's presence.

Sin and guilt will keep you out of God's presence and out of His blessing, but His mercy and His grace are extended toward you today. The next step is yours!

ELEVEN
STAY HUNGRY and THIRSTY for GOD

John 7:37-39 Vs. 37 *In the last day, that great day of the feast, Jesus stood and cried, saying, If any man thirst, let him come unto me, and drink.* Vs. 38 *He that believeth on me, as the scripture hath said, out of his belly shall flow rivers of living water.* Vs. 39 *(But this spake he of the Spirit, which they that believe on him should receive: for the Holy Ghost was not yet given; because that Jesus was not yet glorified.)*

In verse 37, the phrase "if any man thirst" means that this is something we must do. As the Psalmist said, "As the deer panteth for the water, so my soul longeth after Thee" (Psalms 42.1). Are you hungry for all that Jesus has for you or are you satisfied where you are?

Smith Wigglesworth (the great English evangelist) used to say that the only thing he was satisfied with was the fact that he was dissatisfied with where he was.

God has more for you! The Bible says to taste and see that the Lord is good (Psalms 34:8).

Verse 37 above goes on to say, *Let him come unto me and drink.* This is not talking about drinking natural water, but *spiritual water.*

One of the interesting things about this passage is the very next verse where He says that *out of your innermost being shall flow rivers of living water.* That *living water* He is talking about is the Holy Ghost.

First you hunger and thirst from your heart and then the river of God comes. "Out of your belly shall flow rivers of life-giving water."

It is so important that we stay hungry and thirsty FOR ALL THAT GOD HAS and that we never get to a place in our lives where we feel we've arrived.

I am *hungrier today* than I have ever been. I am *thirstier today* than I have ever been. *More of Jesus, less of me! I must decrease, but He must increase.*

Let's get rid of other things that would satisfy us and press in for all that God has.

TWELVE
BEING *a* DOER *of* THE WORD

James 1:22-25 (Amp) Vs. 22 *But be doers of the Word [obey the message], and not merely listeners to it, betraying yourselves [into deception by reasoning contrary to the Truth].* Vs. 23 *For if anyone only listens to the Word without obeying it and being a doer of it, he is like a man who looks carefully at his [own] natural face in a mirror;*

Vs. 24 *For he thoughtfully observes himself, and then goes off and promptly forgets what he was like.* Vs. 25 *But he who looks carefully into the faultless law, the [law] of liberty, and is faithful to it and perseveres in looking into it, being not a heedless listener who forgets but an active doer [who obeys], he shall be blessed in his doing (his life of obedience).*

What amazes me more than anything else is that some people would rather live in darkness than come to the light of God's Word and be set free. The worst form of deception is self-deception. This self-deception comes to those who *hear* the Word, but will not be *doers* of the Word.

Every week, churches are full of people who *hear* the Word, but do not *apply* it in their lives. When they walk out of church, they step into their world of unreality—a make-believe world. God's Word is not just something to hear in church; it must also be applied in our daily lives.

God's Word covers every area of our existence here on earth, our marriage and relationships, forgiveness and walking in

God's love, and repentance and restitution. If we want to be blessed in every area of our lives, we must take God at His Word—whatever He says we should do, ***do it!*** We must begin to behave like the Word says we should behave.

You need to receive what God's Word is saying to you and say, "God's Word is talking to *me*. How can I change? How can I apply this to my life?" Before the day is over, make sure you are *doing* God's Word. If you took just *one* principle a *week* and applied it in your life, changing in that area, at the end of one year, 52 things would have been changed in your life.

You can hear God's Word, you can even talk about God's Word all the time, but until you do it and live it, you are living a lie. I don't know about you, but this one thing I do know: God cannot bless a lie. God can only bless the truth.

Make a decision today to act on God's Word and be a *doer* of the Word and not a *hearer* only. Don't be *self-deceived*. This is not what you would want in your life, because deception will lead to destruction and, ultimately, death.

Don't say to yourself, "This Word is for other people." Say, "This Word is for *me!* I must *obey* the Word of God and *do* it!" The rewards of becoming a *doer* of God's Word are *blessings and abundant life!*

THIRTEEN
THE CAUSE *of* REVIVAL

Revival and its causes have been studied and discussed for years by many different people, but *revival simply begins in your heart.* Revival does not begin in your spouse's heart; it begins in you. And until revival begins in you, it's never going to begin in someone else.

You cannot experience revival if you are spiritually dead. Some Christians are as cold as a corpse. When they walk into a room, the spiritual temperature drops ten degrees, because they're part of "the frozen chosen."

If you're on fire for God and you're full of the Holy Spirit, you can take the power of God wherever you go. But too many Christians are allowing the influence of the world to stop them or pull them down.

Again, revival begins in your heart. Ezekiel said:

Ezekiel 36:26, 27 *A new heart also will I give you, and a new spirit will I put within you: and I will take the stony heart out of your flesh, and I will give you an heart of flesh. And I will put my spirit within you . . .*

Some people need a new spirit; that is, the Spirit of God needs to revive them. They sit like a bump on a log in the Sunday morning service, jumping up between yawns to shout, "Amen!"

Revival brings a change of heart. When you have been revived, you will go and change other people's hearts—not their heads. God doesn't want fat heads; He wants fat hearts. There are enough fat heads going around! It isn't enough just to change your mind; you must have a change of heart. That's what happens when you are born again—you have a change of heart.

Some of you are not experiencing revival right now because you need a change of heart. If you will let the Spirit of God move in your life, He will give you a change of heart, and you will be in revival. Then people will look at you and say, "Everyone's talking about revival, but that person is *walking* in it."

You can have revival all the time. You can have revival in your home. You can have revival in your car as you're commuting to work at six o'clock on a Monday morning. You can have revival in the midst of adverse circumstances. Peace is not the absence of war, but the presence of God. Therefore, you can have the peace of God and the presence of God in the middle of war.

When a wave of revival comes, it comes with such power that it always stirs up everything in its path. When you look inside a barrel that's filled with rainwater, it looks like it contains clean water. But if you take a stick and start stirring it, you'll stir up the sediment that is on the bottom. The water that looked clean is actually dirty and full of muck!

You'll know when revival has hit, because it will affect every area of society at the same time. The Word of God is the same to the rich man as to the poor man. We're all poor without the Lord Jesus. Therefore, revival will reach out not only to the doctors and lawyers, but also down into the gutter among the drunkards, prostitutes, and street people.

FOURTEEN
STANDING *in* THE STORMS *of* LIFE

James 1:2-4 (Amp) Vs. 2 *Consider it wholly joyful, my brethren, whenever you are enveloped in or encounter trials of any sort or fall into various temptations. Vs. 3 Be assured and understand that the trial and proving of your faith bring out endurance and steadfastness and patience.*

Vs. 4 *But let endurance and steadfastness and patience have full play and do a thorough work, so that you may be [people] perfectly and fully developed [with no defects], lacking in nothing.*

I have heard people say that if you do the will of God, the devil doesn't like it and will come against you to stop you. But then I have heard the same people say that if things go wrong in your life, it is because you have opened the door to the devil. Well, which one is it? What we need to realize is that there are only two times the devil will attack you — when you are doing something *wrong* and when you are doing something *right*.

That may make you feel a little discouraged, but what you will come to see, if you have not already, is that tests and trials come to *everybody* in life. How we act *in the midst* of a negative situation determines our outcome, whether good or bad. You see, even though the devil means to hurt you, God can turn every situation around and bring something good out of it. The Bible says, *Many evils confront the [consistently] righteous, but the Lord delivers him out of them all.* **(Psalms 34:19 Amp)** *And call on Me in the day of trouble; I will* *deliver you, and you shall honor and glorify Me.* **(Psalms 50:15 Amp)**

If you come to realize that your troubles are caused by your own disobedience and that you are outside the will of God, then you need to make the necessary adjustments, repent, and change.

When you are in the will of God, you can *stand* in the middle of the storms of life, *rebuke* the adverse circumstances in the Name of Jesus, and say, "I am not quitting—God is on my side and He will see me through!"

If you never faced tests and trials, how would you know if you really have what it takes to stand under pressure? For it is only under pressure that you find out what you are made of. You must first squeeze a grape to get the *juice.*

The Bible says in **James 1:12:** *Blessed (happy, to be envied) is the man who is patient under trial and stands up under temptation, for when he has stood the test and been approved, he will receive [the victor's] crown of life which God has promised to those who love Him.*

There is a victor's crown waiting for all who stand before the Lord on that day, knowing they have been faithful and have stood firm through all the storms of life.

FIFTEEN

BREAKING *the* CURSE *of* POVERTY

III John verse 2 (Amp) *Beloved, I pray that you may prosper in every way and [that your body] may keep well, even as [I know] your soul keeps well and prospers.*

In the church world as a whole, the word *prosperity* has been interpreted as being a *bad* word, but in the Bible it is actually a good word. The word *salvation* comes from the Greek word *sozo*, which means soundness, wholeness, healing, preservation, deliverance, and prosperity. To *prosper* means to be *abundantly supplied.*

All the goodness of God is wrapped up in our salvation, through the finished work of Jesus on the cross of Calvary. When Jesus died on the cross and rose again, He not only paid the price for our sin and sickness, but also for our provision. God's goal in sending Jesus was that everything Adam had lost would be restored to him. The very first miracle Jesus did in Cana of Galilee, when He turned the water into wine, was a miracle of provision. What was He saying by this miracle? He was saying, "I can take care of the very least thing in your life; I am all you need."

Psalms 37:25 (Amp) *I have been young and now am old, yet have I not seen the [uncompromisingly] righteous forsaken or their seed begging bread.*

God *wants* to bless us, but we have to get rid of the "poverty mentality" that says God does not want us blessed, He wants us poor. That is a lie from the pit of hell. Everything in God's creation speaks of His provision. The stars, the sea, the mountains, the flowers—God spared no expense. Why would He now have His people, His children, live on earth with *nothing*—with lack in their lives? Psalms 23:1 says, *The Lord is my shepherd, I SHALL NOT WANT.* God *wants* to bless us—because He loves us so much.

Some people might say, "Well, Brother Rodney, prosperity will ruin you." But the Bible says in Proverbs 1:32 that prosperity ruins the *fool*. The issue is not whether or not God *wants* to bless us; that is an established Bible fact. He *does* want to bless us. The issue is whether or not God can *trust* us with His blessing.

I want you to make the decision today to break the curse of poverty off your lives and families. Decide not only to accept Jesus as your *Savior* and *Healer*, but also accept Him as your *Provider*.

SIXTEEN
WATCH *your* MOUTH *and* SAY WHAT *the* BIBLE SAYS ABOUT YOU

Proverbs 4:20-27 (Amp) Vs. 20 *My son, attend to my words; consent and submit to my sayings.* Vs. 21 *Let them not depart from your sight; keep them in the center of your heart.* Vs. 22 *For they are life to those who find them, healing and health to all their flesh.*

Vs. 23 *Keep and guard your heart with all vigilance and above all that you guard, for out of it flow the springs of life.* Vs. 24 *Put away from you false and dishonest speech, and willful and contrary talk put far from you.*

Vs. 25 *Let your eyes look right on [with fixed purpose], and let your gaze be straight before you.* Vs. 26 *Consider well the path of your feet, and let all your ways be established and ordered aright.* Vs. 27 *Turn not aside to the right hand nor to the left; remove your foot from evil.*

Philemon 1:6 (Amp) *[And I pray] that the participation in and sharing of your faith may produce and promote full recognition and appreciation and understanding and precise knowledge of every good [thing] that is ours in [our identification with] Christ Jesus [and unto His glory].*

Proverbs 18:20, 21 (Amp) *Vs. 20 A man's [moral] self shall be filled with the fruit of his mouth; and with the consequence of his* *words he must be satisfied [whether good or evil].*

Vs. 21 *Death and life are in the power of the tongue, and they who indulge in it shall eat the fruit of it [for death or life].*

James 1:8 (Amp) *[For being as he is] a man of two minds (hesitating, dubious, irresolute), [he is] unstable and unreliable and uncertain about everything [he thinks, feels, decides].*

1. I am a child of God - Rom. 8:16
2. I am not my own – I am bought with a price - I Cor. 6:19, 20
3. I am crucified with Christ - Gal. 2:20
4. I am dead with Christ - Col. 3:3
5. I am buried with Christ - Col. 2:12
6. I am risen with Christ - Col. 2:13
7. I am a new creature - II Cor. 5:17
8. I am a partaker of His divine nature - II Peter 1:4
9. I am delivered from the powers of darkness - Col.1:13
10. I am translated into the Kingdom of His dear Son - Col. 1:13
11. I am a Son of God and I am led by His Spirit - Rom. 8:14
12. I am protected by the hands of angels wherever I go - Ps. 91:11
13. I am casting all my cares upon Him because He cares for me - I Pet. 5:7
14. I am strong in the Lord and in the power of His might - Eph. 6:10
15. I am doing all things through Christ who strengthens me - Phil. 4:13
16. I am delighting myself in the Lord - Ps. 37:4
17. I am blessed coming in and going out - Deut. 28:6
18. I am blessed with all spiritual blessings - Eph. 1:3
19. I am healed by the stripes Jesus bore for me - I Pet. 2:24

20. I am reigning in life by one, Jesus Christ - Rom. 5:17
21. I am walking by faith and not by sight - II Cor. 5:7
22. I am casting down vain imaginations - II Cor. 10:4, 5
23. I am bringing every thought captive - II Cor. 10:5
24. I am the righteousness of God in Him - II Cor. 5:21
25. I am complete in Him - Col. 2:10
26. I am quick to listen, slow to speak, and slow to wrath - James 1:19
27. I am set free from the law of sin and death - Rom. 8:2
28. I am delivered from the fear of death - Heb. 2:15
29. I am laboring to enter His rest - Heb. 4:11
30. I am boldly entering the throne of grace in my time of need - Heb. 4:16
31. I am walking in the Spirit, not fulfilling the lusts of the flesh - Gal. 5:16
32. I am glorifying God in my body and in my spirit, which are God's - I Cor. 6:20
33. I am saved and so is my household - Acts 16:31
34. I am walking in newness of life - Rom. 6:4
35. I am an imitator of God - Eph. 5:1
36. I am rooted and grounded in love - Eph. 3:17
37. I am being transformed by the renewing of my mind - Rom 12:1, 2
38. I am fixing my eyes on what is eternal - II Cor. 4:18
39. I am more than a conqueror - Rom. 8:37
40. I am receiving power from the Lord to get wealth - Deut. 8:18
41. I am growing up into Jesus Christ in all things - Eph. 4:15
42. I am speaking the truth in love - Eph. 4:15
43. I am an heir of God and joint heirs with Jesus - Rom. 8:17
44. I am acknowledging Him in all things - Prov. 3:6
45. I am His sheep, He is my Shepherd - Ps. 23:1
46. I am His workmanship - Eph. 2:10
47. I am saved by grace through faith - Eph. 2:8
48. I am washed - I Cor. 6:11

49. I am forgiven - Col. 1:13, 14
50. I am delivered from the hand of the enemy - Ps. 107:2

In a day and age when people are so ready to believe the lies of the devil through what others say about them, what they read in papers and magazines, and see on television, it is important that we find out what God's Word says about us and that we say what God's Words says about us.

I AM what the Word says I AM.

SEVENTEEN
LIVE LONG- LIVE HEALTHY- DO *it* GOD'S WAY

Proverbs 3:1-8 (Amp)   Vs. 1 *My son, forget not my law or teaching, but let your heart keep my commandments;* Vs. 2 *For length of days and years of a life [worth living] and tranquility [inward and outward and continuing through old age till death], these shall they add to you.*

Vs. 3 *Let not mercy and kindness [shutting out all hatred and selfishness] and truth [shutting out all deliberate hypocrisy or falsehood] forsake you; bind them about your neck, write them upon the tablet of your heart.* Vs. 4 *So shall you find favor, good understanding, and high esteem in the sight [or judgment] of God and man.*

Vs. 5 *Lean on, trust in, and be confident in the Lord with all your heart and mind and do not rely on your own insight or understanding.*   Vs. 6 *In all your ways know, recognize, and acknowledge Him, and He will direct and make straight and plain your paths.*

Vs. 7 *Be not wise in your own eyes; reverently fear and worship the Lord and turn [entirely] away from evil.* Vs. 8 *It shall be health to your nerves and sinews, and marrow and moistening to your bones.*

There are certain things that all of us want in our lives, whether we are a child of God or not. We want to live a good, long life with good health and favor and respect from others. Well, there is a way to have all these things in our lives, but they don't come by the choices we make by ourselves or by following the advice of the "experts" of this world. Long life, health and favor come from one place alone — God's Word.

John 1:1 (Amp) *In the beginning [before all time] was the Word (Christ), and the Word was with God, and the Word was God Himself.* God says that if we have His Word and keep His commandments, we will live a long life, improve our health, and have our needs met. Not only does God promise us a *long* life if we obey His Word and put it into our hearts, but He promises us a great *quality* of life, too.

We need to have *confidence* in God and His Word — more than in our own thoughts or ability. Our own understanding is very limited. We only know what we have been taught, but we don't know our future and we don't always know right from wrong. God knows everything and He is our ultimate standard. The world says, "Do whatever *feels* good." But sometimes what *feels* good to us is not always the right thing. *God knows* what is *right* for our lives. We need His wisdom and insight to direct us.

Proverbs 14:12 (Amp) *There is a way which seems right to a man and appears straight before him, but at the end of it is the way of death.*

We need to make God and His Word part of everything we do. If we recognize and acknowledge Him in all our ways, He will make our paths straight and plain. Without God, our daily survival is a struggle — on the job, in our homes, in our relationships, in our finances. But when we commit to follow the Lord in everything, when we make Him part of every decision, then He will make our lives flow smoothly.

When God is in control — there is no confusion in our lives — we can see clearly — we know where we are going.

We must not be wise in our own eyes. Pride will stop us from submitting to God's Word. Humbly allowing God to lead us and correct us will bring us long life and all of His blessings. Don't let anything stand in the way of allowing God to have His way in your life.

EIGHTEEN
A REVIVAL GREATER *than* PENTECOST

Acts 2:1-6 (Amp) Vs. 1 *And when the day of Pentecost had fully come, they were all assembled together in one place,* Vs. 2 *When suddenly there came a sound from heaven like the rushing of a violent tempest blast, and it filled the whole house in which they were sitting.*

Vs. 3 *And there appeared to them tongues resembling fire, which were separated and distributed and which settled on each one of them.* Vs. 4 *And they were all filled (diffused throughout their souls) with the Holy Spirit and began to speak in other (different, foreign) languages (tongues), as the Spirit kept giving them clear and loud expression [in each tongue in appropriate words].*

Vs. 5 *Now there were then residing in Jerusalem Jews, devout and God-fearing men from every country under heaven.* Vs. 6 *And when this sound was heard, the multitude came together and they were astonished and bewildered, because each one heard them [the apostles] speaking in his own [particular] dialect.*

When the wind of God blew into the Upper Room filling its occupants with the Holy Spirit, they began to speak in other tongues. They were so overcome by the Holy Spirit that the people thought they were drunk on wine. This experience was totally foreign to the natural, carnal minds of the observers. Of course, it was a new experience to the 120 also, but they were open and waiting for the move of God and the outpouring of the Holy Spirit, even though they had no idea what would take place until it happened.

The sad thing is, many today who have received Jesus as Lord and Savior still don't know who the Holy Spirit is, nor do they understand how He works. But a great, new, wonderful outpouring of the Spirit of God is about to take place and believers will have a greater revelation of Him. We are on the brink of an outbreak of the Holy Spirit *greater* than the one that came on the Day of Pentecost. Why do I say it will it be greater? Because we're not starting this dispensation, we're wrapping it up! The wind of the Holy Spirit will come in this day and hour and blow upon the dry bones of the Church of the Lord Jesus Christ. Can these bones live again? Yes, with the mighty wind of the Spirit of God that will come in this day, these bones *can* live again.

Winds of revival are beginning to blow from the north, the south, the east, and the west into many different denominations and groups. The Holy Spirit is not a respecter of persons. He answers the hungry who come to Him and say, "O God, we would seek your face. We would see your glory. Come and breathe upon us. Let your fire fall upon me, O God! Let your Spirit burn within my heart. Bring about a change in my life."

The glory of God will not fall on only 120 people, as it did in the Upper Room; it will fall upon millions and millions of people! God will breathe upon the blood-bought Church — the called-out ones — and they will rise up and go forth like a mighty army. God wants to prepare His Church for this end-time revival. How can we prepare ourselves for revival? We must get our hearts right by repenting of any sin in our lives and humbling ourselves under His mighty hand. When we open our hearts and yield to the Holy Spirit like this, the glory of God will come, and true manifestations of the Holy Spirit will be present in our meetings.

We must learn to recognize the anointing of the Spirit of God and begin to flow with Him. We can know when He's in a meeting and when He's not. When His anointing is *not* there, don't try to make something happen, because if you do, you mock and grieve Him! We just need to seek Jesus and His will and purpose for our lives and be open for Him to do whatever He wants to do. We don't try to *make* something happen, but we don't *stop* whatever God begins to do in us, either. We simply allow the Holy Spirit to have His way in our lives. It is only as we *die* to the things of our fleshly, carnal nature that we can be *resurrected* into the newness of life that Jesus made possible for us.

Matthew 10:39 (Amp) *Whoever finds his [lower] life will lose it [the higher life], and whoever loses his [lower] life on My account will find it [the higher life].*

NINETEEN

THE JOY *of* OUR SALVATION

Psalms 51:9-13 Vs. 9 *Hide thy face from my sins, and blot out all mine iniquities.* Vs. 10 *Create in me a clean heart, O God; and renew a right spirit within me.* Vs. 11 *Cast me not away from thy presence; and take not thy holy spirit from me.*

Vs. 12 *Restore unto me the joy of thy salvation; and uphold me with thy free spirit.* Vs. 13 *Then will I teach transgressors thy ways; and sinners shall be converted unto thee.*

Even the Old Covenant saints understood salvation. They realized that they needed a completely new heart, that they needed their spirit to be completely renewed (born again, as Jesus put it). They understood that the coming Messiah would make this feat possible. Even though they could not participate in this salvation in their lifetime, they longed for it and they knew *joy* in the salvation that they did have. Their sins were covered by the blood of bulls and goats and they were counted righteous because of their faith in God. How much more do we have reason to *rejoice* in our *salvation*.

We have the *fulfillment* of the promise of God! We can experience the clean heart and the right spirit in our own lives. And yet, even though we have participated in this wonderful salvation that the Old Covenant saints longed for, many times we take it for granted. We do not appreciate it as we should, or we take advantage of it—we just outright abuse it.

We need to realize the wonderful thing that happened to us at the new birth—at the time we repented of sin and accepted Jesus as Lord and Savior, believing that He died and rose again to pay for our sin. We were absolutely and completely *changed*. A wonderful miracle took place in us and instantaneously our hearts changed. We were dead to God one moment and on our way to hell (if we died in our sin, that's where we would find ourselves). At the time of the new birth, our spirit becomes alive in God and the life and nature of God is re-created within our spirit. If our physical bodies were to die at that moment, our spirit would leave and instantly be with our Lord.

This wonderful salvation, which literally means soundness, healing, deliverance and preservation, was bought at a very high cost. Our Father planned the whole thing long before Adam even existed. He visited men and made covenants with them through the years. When the time was right, He sent His only begotten Son from heaven to earth to be born in human form, to experience everything in person that we experience (yet He was without sin). He had to go through all the temptations we face—but He could not give in or succumb to sin or all would be lost.

He had to lay down His life and die a cruel and painful death, enduring physical and mental abuse and torment. And on top of that, He had to experience sin, sickness, and torment as He took it upon Himself and carried it into the grave for us. He, Who had never been separated from His Father, had to endure a separation from God. *My God, my God, why hast thou forsaken me?* **(Matthew 27:46)** But, thank God, because He was sinless and innocent, the grave could not keep Him. His Father cried, "It is enough!" and resurrected Him from the dead with the keys of death, hell and the grave. The devil was forever defeated and stripped of his power to condemn men to hell.

Psalms 13: 5, 6 *But I have trusted in thy mercy; my heart shall rejoice in thy salvation. I will sing unto the Lord, because he hath dealt bountifully with me.*

How can we take for granted this great salvation that was purchased by the precious blood of Jesus, the Lamb of God? How can we be sad or depressed when we have the life of God living in us? We have His grace and His mercy! Even though we go through hard times, we can *rejoice* in our *salvation* because we have His grace and mercy working on our behalf!

TWENTY
SEVEN REDEMPTIVE NAMES *of* GOD

Under the Old Covenant, God revealed Himself through seven redemptive names. As we study these names, we discover His character. All seven Old Covenant names are fulfilled and brought together in one New Covenant name—the name of Jesus.

Number One - JEHOVAH JIREH "The Lord will Provide" — Genesis 22:1-14 This passage tells the story of Abraham preparing to sacrifice Isaac, according to God's instructions. God saw that Abraham was obedient, so He sent an angel to stop him from killing Isaac. He provided a ram, caught in a thicket, for Abraham to sacrifice instead. Abraham called the place *Jehovah Jireh*—the Lord will provide. In the New Covenant, we see this name fulfilled through the person of the Lord Jesus in Philippians 4:19.

Number Two - JEHOVAH NISSI "The Lord our Banner" — Exodus 17:8-15 This passage tells the story of a battle between Israel and Amalek at Rephidim. Moses went to the top of the hill with the rod of God. As long as he held his hands in the air, Israel prevailed, but when his hands fell, Amalek prevailed. Aaron and Hur seated Moses on a rock and helped to hold up his hands, and Israel won the battle. Afterwards, Moses built an altar and called it *Jehovah Nissi*—the Lord is my banner. In the New Covenant, Jesus says in John 15:13 that there is no greater love than to lay down your life for a friend. His banner over us is love.

Number Three - JEHOVAH SHALOM "The Lord is our Peace" — Judges 6:24 The Lord called Gideon to serve Him and gave him a sign to show that He was with him and that he had found favor in His sight. Afterward, Gideon built an altar and called it *Jehovah Shalom* – the Lord our Peace. In the New Covenant, we see this fulfilled in Ephesians 2:14: *Jesus is our peace.*

Number Four - JEHOVAH ROHI "The Lord is our Shepherd" — Psalm 23:1-6 In this passage we see the Lord our Shepherd-the One who leads beside the still waters. He restores my soul; He restores my life. The Shepherd cares for us and even gives His life for the sheep. We see *Jehovah Rohi* in Jesus in John 10:11.

Number Five - JEHOVAH TSIDKENU "The Lord our Righteousness" — Jeremiah 23:5, 6 God says, through the prophet Jeremiah, that He is going to raise a righteous branch out of the line of David. He will reign as King and do wisely and execute justice and righteousness. His name will be *The Lord our Righteousness.* We see that Jesus has been made our righteousness in I Corinthians 1:30.

Number Six - JEHOVAH SHAMMAH "The Lord is Present" — Ezekiel 48:35 The prophet Ezekiel, speaking of the New Jerusalem (The City Foursquare), says that the city will be called "The Lord is There" or "The Lord is Present." Hebrews 13:5 says, "I will never leave you nor forsake you." Jesus is present always.

Number Seven - JEHOVAH ROPHE "The Lord thy Physician" — Exodus 15:26 God says in Exodus, *I am the Lord that healeth thee – I am your Physician.* Many people believe that God *can* heal them, but they are not sure that He *will* heal them or that He *wants* to heal them. Under the Old Covenant, He said, *I am the Lord that healeth thee.* James 5:15 says that the prayer of faith shall save the sick and the Lord will raise them up.

Through these seven Names, we see the character of God displayed. It is exciting to know that all these Names are fulfilled in ONE Name — **JESUS.**

TWENTY-ONE
A SIGN SPOKEN AGAINST

Luke 2:34, 35 (Amp) *And Simeon blessed them and said to Mary His mother, Behold, this Child is appointed and destined for the fall and rising of many in Israel, and for a sign that is spoken against – And a sword will pierce through your own soul also-that the secret thoughts and purposes of many hearts may be brought out and disclosed.*

These words were spoken by the aged Simeon as he held the long-promised Savior in his arms. After 30 years had transpired, this prophecy was fulfilled when Jesus stood in the synagogue at Nazareth to read. With the scroll of the Prophet Isaiah in His Hand, He read, "The Spirit of the Lord is upon me," and He said, "Today is this scripture fulfilled in your ears." They reacted violently to His words and even tried to throw Him over a cliff, but He turned and walked through them and went on His way.

Jesus became the sign spoken against so that the very thoughts of people's hearts might be revealed. *God will offend the mind to reveal the heart.* The moving of the Holy Spirit, like that of the ministry of Jesus, will always uncover and draw out into the open the antagonism of the carnal mind, which is enmity against God.

The reason certain people oppose the moving of the Spirit is because they are ignorant of the Spirit's moving, or perhaps it is because they have seen excesses (people going beyond the boundaries of the move of the Spirit). The Pharisees were offended because Jesus healed on the Sabbath; they were offended because His disciples would not ceremonially wash their hands when they ate.

It would be easy to compromise and fit into the *status quo* of religious tradition and be held captive by the fear of man. Just because there are so-called "excesses" according to the opinion of men, should we stop the real thing? Should the early church not have sold anything else, ever, because of Ananias and Sapphira? No, but they sure learned not to lie to the Holy Ghost. Should they have stopped celebrating the Lord's Supper because of the excesses at Corinth? Certainly not!

When drought has plagued the land for a time and then rain begins to pour down and then to flood, sweeping away everything, bringing much harm and damage, do we speak out about the evils of the abundance of rain? There are always people who desire revival until it comes, and then bitterly oppose it because it does not meet their criteria. Perhaps the instrument God used, through whom the blessing flowed, was not what their convictions had led them to expect.

Some people warn from Matthew 24:24 that satanic agents are going to deceive by signs and wonders. If this reasoning is correct, does that mean that God no longer does signs and wonders (if we read our Bibles correctly, we will see that He has done them in the past) and only the devil has the monopoly in the supernatural realm? Is the devil able to manifest himself to us, but God cannot? Certainly not! Must the Moseses and Aarons of the last days hold their rods idle, while the magicians of Egypt cast theirs down and turn them into serpents? God is certainly more powerful than the devil!

The children of God have *more* power available to them than the children of the devil. As Moses' rod changed to a serpent and swallowed up the magicians' rods, we should see, in these last days, the power of God — stronger than the power of the devil.

I John 4:4 *. . . greater is he that is in you, than he that is in the world.* The *signs and wonders* manifested in the last days and the *move of the Holy Spirit* might offend the religious Pharisees of this age, but they also will *reveal* what's in their *hearts* as they *speak against* them.

TWENTY-TWO
THE SUDDENLIES *of* GOD

Acts 2:1-4 *And when the day of Pentecost was fully come, they were all with one accord in one place. And suddenly there came a sound from heaven as of a rushing mighty wind, and it filled all the house where they were sitting. And there appeared unto them cloven tongues like as of fire, and it sat upon each of them. And they were all filled with the Holy Ghost, and began to speak with other tongues, as the Spirit gave them utterance.*

Verse 2 says, "*Suddenly* . . ." It is interesting to note that even though they were *waiting* for the coming of the Holy Spirit and they were *expecting* the Holy Spirit to be poured out, when He came it was a *suddenly* experience. God has a way of surprising us. Even though we may be waiting for Him, He often makes Himself real to us, or makes His presence known to us, in an unexpected way. Many times we think we have figured out how God is going to meet our need. We can list ten ways we think He is going to do it—and then He comes through with the eleventh way at two seconds to midnight. He surprises us. These are the "*suddenlies*" of God.

Are you in a situation where you are waiting on God for a breakthrough in certain areas of your life? If you are, then I want you to be encouraged. God knows exactly what you need and He has ways to meet those needs.

Trust Him implicitly for *everything* in your life. Jesus told the disciples to tarry in Jerusalem, and wait for the coming of the Holy Spirit. They did not know what to expect, waiting in that upper room, because they did not know what the Holy Spirit looked like. But when He came — it was SUDDENLY — like a rushing mighty wind, which filled the house. The fire of God fell upon them. No one could doubt. He had arrived!

When God comes through for you, it will be so evident that He has had the whole thing planned from the beginning that you will feel ashamed for worrying and not trusting Him from the start. Do not look at the natural — to what we can see with our eyes and perceive with our senses — but anticipate the "*suddenlies*" of God.

Never give up, for your answer may be right around the corner. Corners are interesting things — you cannot see around them until you get right up to them. Do not worry that you cannot see your answer right here, right now. God has you in the palm of His hand and if you will trust Him and not lose heart before you reach the corner, you will see the answer. SUDDENLY your answer will be there, your need will be met, the right door will open for you!

Expect the unexpected! SUDDENLY — your God will come through for you!

TWENTY-THREE
AS *a* MAN THINKS, SO *is* HE

GOOD HEART — GOOD MOUTH   GOOD WORDS — GOOD FRUIT
BAD HEART — BAD MOUTH   BAD WORDS — BAD FRUIT
THE MOUTH SPEAKS WHAT IS IN THE HEART

Luke 6:43-45 *For a good tree bringeth not forth corrupt fruit; neither doth a corrupt tree bring forth good fruit. For every tree is known by his own fruit. For of thorns men do not gather figs, nor of a bramble bush gather they grapes. A good man out of the good treasure of his heart bringeth forth that which is good; and an evil man out of the evil treasure of his heart bringeth forth that which is evil: for of the abundance of the heart his mouth speaketh.*

If you want to find out what is on the inside of a person, spend some time with that person. You will see what they are full of, for it will come out the moment they open their mouth.

A man with a good heart will speak good things and the man with an evil heart will speak evil things. If you are a critical person, then criticism will come out of your mouth.

Matthew 5:28 *But I say unto you, That whosoever looketh on a woman to lust after her hath committed adultery with her already in his heart.*

We have to realize that God looks on the heart, so sins of the heart are very important. If an individual lusts in his heart over another, then according to the Word, it is the same as though he actually commits adultery.

Proverbs 4:23, 24 *Keep thy heart with all diligence; for out of it are the issues of life. Put away from thee a froward mouth, and perverse lips put far from thee.*

According to scripture, we need to protect our heart with all diligence, for out of it flow the issues of life.

Ephesians 4:29 *Let no corrupt communication proceed out of your mouth, but that which is good to the use of edifying, that it may minister grace unto the hearers.*

Don't allow corrupt communication to proceed out of your mouth, but only that which is good for edification.

Colossians 4:6 *Let your speech be always with grace, seasoned with salt, that ye may know how ye ought to answer every man.*

Let your speech be seasoned with salt. Put a guard over your mouth and protect your heart and, if need be, allow the Lord to take out the stony heart and put in a heart of flesh.

Psalm 45:1 *My heart is inditing a good matter: I speak of the things which I have made touching the king: my tongue is the pen of a ready writer.*

Allow God to make your tongue as the pen of a ready writer, that you might become an oracle of God, God's mouthpiece to a lost and dying world.

TWENTY-FOUR
A SPECK *and* A BEAM

Luke 6:41, 42 *And why beholdest thou the mote that is in thy brother's eye, but perceivest not the beam that is in thine own eye? Either how canst thou say to thy brother, Brother, let me pull out the mote that is in thine eye, when thou thyself beholdest not the beam that is in thine own eye? Thou hypocrite, cast out first the beam out of thine own eye, and then shalt thou see clearly to pull out the mote that is in thy brother's eye.*

Many times it is easy to judge your brother and forget to judge yourself. You can see a speck in his eye but forget the beam in your own eye. How many people judge themselves by their intentions and judge others by their actions? It is so important that we always remember that every time we point a finger at someone else, we have three pointing back at ourselves.

In the early days of my ministry in South Africa, I spent time with a leading minister in our nation. Every time we got together he and his friends would sit and criticize everyone. I thought this was acceptable, so being young and impressionable at the time, I fell into the trap of the enemy. I also remember, however, that I would go away from a luncheon with them feeling dirty, grieved, and saddened in my heart. I knew that we should not have been doing this, as it was not pleasing to the Lord Jesus.

When I left South Africa for a period of time and had little or no communication with these people, God began to do a work in my heart. I made a decision to focus on my own "beam" and deal with it, and leave other people's "specks" alone. Three years later I met up with the minister once again. Nothing had changed. He and his friends were still critical of everyone they knew. It seemed as if no one could measure up to their standards. The only problem is that their standards seemed to be different for every person.

I had not realized how deeply I had been involved in the "speck ministry" previously, failing to look at the beam in my own eye, until I heard this minister being critical again. This time I did not join in, but to my own amazement I found myself saying to him that I was not going to criticize others. I explained that I was too busy trying to make sure that I obeyed God and did nothing to grieve Him.

The minister was visibly upset with me because I would not join in the criticism of others. I was surprised (and relieved) to find that in the three years of being apart I had changed so much. I did not want to go back to *speck-u-lating* anymore! God had set me free when I made a decision to focus on the beam *I* had.

The Lord does not say we cannot help our brother deal with his speck, but we must first make sure we have dealt with whatever stands in *our* way, whatever hinders us.

Be careful not to criticize or judge, but walk humbly before the Lord, and God's blessing will rest upon your life in a powerful way.

TWENTY-FIVE
THE LAND *of* THE FREE *and* THE HOME *of* THE BRAVE

Psalm 33:12 *Blessed is the nation whose God is the LORD; and the people whom he hath chosen for his own inheritance.*

This great land of the United States of America was founded because of man's desire to be free and to have religious freedom. In this land, one can have a dream and see that dream become a reality, regardless of one's race, color or creed. This is what America stands for, a nation founded by pioneers who braved the winter and the ruggedness of this land to establish what is still known as the greatest country on the face of the earth.

When God called us to America, He said that as America had sown missionaries over the last 200 years, He was going to raise up people from other nations and send them to the United States. He then told us to come and stir up the churches and tell them to get ready for the coming revival. We count it a privilege to be called as missionaries to the USA. We have made America our home and are proud to be Americans, living in the land of opportunity and able to be pioneers, braving new frontiers. Let me share comments made by other pioneers:

SAM WALTER FOSS: Bring me men to match my mountains; bring me men to match my plains – men with empires in their purpose, and new eras in their brains.

HERMAN MELVILLE: America has been settled by a people of all nations; all nations may claim her for their own. We are not a narrow tribe of men. No, our blood is made as the flood of the Amazon, made up of a thousand noble currents, all pouring into one. We are not a nation so much as a world.

GEORGE MAGAR MARDIKIAN: You who have been born in America, I wish I could make you understand what it is like not to have been born an American, not to have been an American all of your life. Then suddenly — with the words of a man in flowing robes — *for that moment and forever after,* you belong with your fathers to a million yesterdays — the next moment you belong to America for a million unborn tomorrows.

CHARLES AUGUSTUS LINDBERGH: What kind of man would live where there is no daring? I don't believe in taking foolish chances, but nothing can be accomplished without taking any chance at all.

WENDALL LEWIS WILKIE: Our way of living together in America is a strong but delicate fabric. It is made up of many threads that have been woven over many centuries by the patience and sacrifice of countless liberty-loving men and women.

AMERICA
By Rodney Howard-Browne

From the harbor brightly shining,
The lady her beacon beams
To all those tired and weary,
Come to freedom's dream.
And now that freedom threatened,
revival her only hope,
America, our time has come
to fulfill your heavenly goal.
From the grandeur of Alaska
to the blue of the Florida Keys,
To the Aloha of the Island,
From Maine it's plain to see fifty nations,
It seems to fill your shores
As weary travelers come to seek
the joy that freedom brings,
And to bask beneath your sun.
The cry my heart desires
As one born out of due time,
The burning cry of revival
from one of your newest sons.
America, America, may your eagle soar again
High above the clouds of darkness,
back into His glory again.

TWENTY-SIX

HISTORY of REVIVAL MINISTRIES INTERNATIONAL'S *annual* SUMMER CAMPMEETING

Through the summer of 1991, we held revival meetings in Louisville, Kentucky, and all over the surrounding area. Near the end of the summer, we decided to rent a facility and hold a "Campmeeting" to bring together the people from the churches in which we had ministered and anyone else who desired to come. This first Campmeeting was held in Jeffersonville, Indiana, just across the Ohio River from Louisville. We had a wonderful four days, registering about 500 people. We decided to make this an annual event.

The next year we moved into the Louisville Convention Center, in a room upstairs that could hold about 1,200 people, registering approximately 800–1000 people. In 1993, we used the same room, but could not fit the people in and had to use an overflow room. About 3,000 people registered. The following year we moved downstairs into the Convention Center's largest room, which could hold 7,500 to 10,000 people. That year we had about 7,500 register. In 1995, we moved Campmeeting to St. Louis, Missouri, at the Kiel Center and registered 13,000 people. In that year, we moved our offices from Louisville, Kentucky, to Tampa, Florida, and decided to move our Campmeeting to Tampa, as well. In 1996, we registered about 10,000.

THE IMPORTANCE *of* CAMPMEETING *to* US AT THE RIVER *at* TAMPA BAY

Hebrews 10:24-25 Vs. 24 *And let us consider one another to provoke unto love and to good works:* Vs. 25 *Not forsaking the assembling of ourselves together, as the manner of some is; but exhorting one another: and so much the more, as ye see the day approaching.*

We at The River believe an event like Campmeeting is important because it is a time we set aside as a church to get totally saturated in revival, and filled with the Holy Ghost. Some of us were touched by revival, but have cooled off—maybe without even realizing it. Some of us don't feel cooled off, but we just need *more*. We need God to do a deeper work in our lives, to keep building on the foundation that has been laid. You may feel that you are in revival now, but if you do not *stay* in Holy Ghost revival meetings, you will not even know if you are on fire or just lukewarm!

When an automobile drives on uneven pavement, its wheels get out of alignment and need to be adjusted. So it is with the human heart—our spirit man. When you have been subjected to the potholes of life, you will need to come into alignment with the Word of God and receive a tune-up in the Spirit. Campmeeting has always been a time of refreshing, allowing God to take us to another level in Him.

TWENTY-SEVEN
RIGHTLY DIVIDING *the* WORD *of* TRUTH

II Timothy 2:15 *Study to show thyself approved unto God, a workman that needeth not to be ashamed, RIGHTLY DIVIDING THE WORD OF TRUTH.*

In this scripture, Paul is instructing Timothy to study the Word of God in order to understand it accurately, to show himself approved unto God, a workman that does not need to be ashamed. It is very evident that scores of Christians have not studied the Word of God thoroughly, because they are confused about what they believe. They may not even realize exactly how confused they are. Many people have taken a little bit of the Old Covenant and a little bit of the New Covenant and put them together to make their own covenant. This covenant is one that puts you in bondage. It is what I call a covenant to nowhere!

The Old Covenant stood as a type and shadow of what was to come. Then the law was given to serve as our schoolmaster, showing us clearly that because we could not keep the law, we needed a mediator—Jesus—between us and God to bring a New Covenant into being.

Hebrews 8:6-8 *Vs. 6 But now hath he obtained a more excellent ministry, by how much also he is the mediator of a better covenant, which was established upon better promises. Vs. 7 For if that first covenant had been faultless, then should no place have been sought for the second. Vs. 8 For finding fault with them, he saith, Behold,* *the days come, saith the Lord, when I will make a new covenant with the house of Israel and with the house of Judah.*

Jesus was the mediator of a better covenant, based upon better promises. The first covenant could never be sufficient, because men were incapable of keeping it. When Jesus cried, "It is finished!" He meant that it was the *end* of the Old Covenant and the *beginning* of the New Covenant.

The **Old** Covenant leads to bondage—the **New** Covenant leads to freedom. The **Old** puts you under the curse, while the **New** brings you into liberty. The **Old** was a dispensation of darkness and fear, tending to bondage—a schoolmaster to bring us to Christ, but very imperfect in comparison to the gospel of the Lord Jesus Christ.

The **New** is a better covenant (vs. 6), a clearer dispensation and discovery of the grace of God to sinners. It requires nothing, but what it promises, grace will perform.

The **New** is based upon better promises, clearer and more express, more spiritual, more absolute. The promises of spiritual and eternal blessings are in this covenant—positive and absolute, along with promises of temporal blessings. These are all linked to the promises of God's Word that if we meet the conditions of His Word, we inherit the promises. All who truly take hold of the New Covenant by faith will always be found preserved by the finished work of the cross.

The **New** was brought about by God's mercy, love, and grace. His wisdom devised it; His Son purchased it; the Holy Spirit brings people into it by the blood, and builds them up in it. The table of the Lord is the meal of the covenant and as we partake, we remember all that was purchased for us. This is why we need to rightly divide the word of truth and not take the **Old Covenant** principles and try to operate them under the **New Covenant**.

Jesus did everything that you and I need in order to live and walk in victory here on earth. All we need to do is come to Him in faith, in simple trust, and say, "Lord Jesus, thank You for all You have done for me. I receive by faith the New Covenant in my life. I rightly divide the word of truth in my life and receive all that heaven has for me." **Let us rightly divide the word of truth.**

TWENTY-EIGHT
NO PRIVATE INTERPRETATION *of* GOD'S WORD

II Peter 1:19-21 Vs. 19 *We have also a more sure word of prophecy; whereunto ye do well that ye take heed, as unto a light that shineth in a dark place, until the day dawn, and the day star arise in your hearts*: Vs. 20 *Knowing this first, that no prophecy of the scripture is of any private interpretation.* Vs. 21 *For the prophecy came not in old time by the will of man: but holy men of God spake as they were moved by the Holy Ghost.*

Through the ages, one of the biggest problems with the way many people read or study the Word of God is that they approach the scriptures believing they can put their own personal and private interpretation on these scriptures. Verse 20 says that *no* prophecy of the scriptures is of any *private* interpretation. People look for a new revelation, something that nobody else has. This causes them to get into error. Cults have their foundation in this loose handling of the scriptures.

II Corinthians 4:2 *But have renounced the hidden things of dishonesty, not walking in craftiness, nor handling the word of God deceitfully; but by manifestation of the truth commending ourselves to every man's conscience in the sight of God.*

We need to realize that if God's Word says something, it is saying the *same* thing to *everyone*. The devil likes to twist the scriptures and get us to question what God has said. "Hath

God said?" He tries to make people doubt God's Word and believe that it is not relevant to our lives today, that it relates to some *other* group of people. Or he will get people to quote God's Word out of context, making it seem to say things that He never actually said.

Let us never use God's Word deceitfully, twisting His Word to condone sin or justify an ungodly lifestyle. I recently heard a prominent minister say that because he was an anointed man of God, he could commit sin and get away with it—that the anointing would cover him. This, dear friends, is deception and error, and he is heading for severe trouble.

If the anointing could not protect David or Samson from trouble because of their sin, then it is not going to cover us in our error and sin. God cannot and will not bless sin. Sin will separate us from God's presence. I cannot stress this enough! Don't ever get some private interpretation of the Word, thinking that you are ahead of everyone and that God has blessed you with some special revelation that nobody else has. This will only lead to separation from God and His presence, and will ultimately lead to destruction and death in your life.

Read God's Word as it is. Don't try to change it or make it say something it doesn't say. Don't read God's Word with religious blinkers and don't try to over-spiritualize the Word. Just take God's Word *as it is,* receive it *as it is,* and *do* what it tells you to do.

TWENTY-NINE
REMEMBER the ONIONS

Numbers 11:4-6 Vs. 4 *And the mixed multitude that was among them fell a-lusting: and the children of Israel also wept again, and said, Who shall give us flesh to eat?* Vs. 5 *We remember the fish, which we did eat in Egypt freely; the cucumbers, and the melons, and the leeks, and the onions, and the garlic:* Vs. 6 *But now our soul is dried away: there is nothing at all, beside this manna, before our eyes.*

Numbers 11:18-20 Vs. 18 *And say thou unto the people, Sanctify yourselves against tomorrow, and ye shall eat flesh: for ye have wept in the ears of the Lord, saying, Who shall give us flesh to eat? For it was well with us in Egypt: therefore the Lord will give you flesh, and ye shall eat.* Vs. 19 *Ye shall not eat one day, nor two days, nor five days, neither ten days, nor twenty days;*

Vs. 20 *But even a whole month, until it come out at your nostrils, and it be loathsome unto you: because that ye have despised the Lord which is among you, and have wept before him, saying, Why came we forth out of Egypt?*

In this passage of scripture, we see something that is all too common, even today. People have a tendency to take God's blessings for granted. They get blasé about the things of God and miss out on the blessings of heaven.

Here, the children of Israel have been delivered out of Egypt and God has provided manna from heaven, but they are complaining. They are saying, "Oh, remember Egypt, the fish, the cucumbers, the leeks and the melons, the onions and the garlic."

In other words — don't forget the onions. Remember the onions.

I have watched people who claim to have been touched by the revival, and who even seem to stay in revival for a while, suddenly begin to go in reverse. It is amazing to see how, after a while, it is as if they begin to say, "Not another day of victory! Not another day of freedom! Not another day of joy! Take us back to Egypt where we had friends and were considered balanced, and the services were normal and we were out of church in an hour and a half." Because of the pull of religion and the flesh, in a moment of pressure, they go back to the slop of the past and lose everything God has done for them.

The children of Israel complained about the manna that God had given them; they wanted onions instead. They complained about the Spirit, wanting the flesh. In this passage, onions represent the flesh. The Israelites wanted and lusted after the past and the flesh.

I am reminded of this humorous account of a man who came home from work and met his wife coming out of the kitchen, crying. His first thought was that the Lord was touching her. He said, "Oh, honey, the anointing, the anointing." To which she replied, "No, dear, not the anointing — the onions, the onions."

Please don't ever look back and long for your Egypt, for the things which once satisfied your flesh. Thank God for your deliverance and for the fact that He has brought you out of bondage into His glorious light. Let us never treat the things of the Spirit as if they are old hat, pulling up our noses at manna from heaven, because we want to keep on remembering the onions.

Let us stay hungry and open for whatever God has for us and not cry for onions when God has given us manna!

THIRTY
FIGHTING the ZUZIMS and ZAMZUMMIMS of LIFE

Genesis 14:5 *And in the fourteenth year came Chedorlaomer, and the kings that were with him, and smote the Rephaims in Ashteroth Karnaim, and the Zuzims in Ham, and the Emims in Shaveh Kiriathaim,*

Deuteronomy 2:20, 21 Vs. 20 *(That also was accounted a land of giants: giants dwelt therein in old time; and the Ammonites call them Zamzummims;* Vs. 21 *A people great, and many, and tall, as the Anakims; but the Lord destroyed them before them; and they succeeded them, and dwelt in their stead:*

Zuzim and Zamzummims are just other names for "giant" — you could put any name in there that might fit the situations of your life. **The giant in your life might be sickness or disease, poverty or fear, marital problems, a sin or habit — something that threatens to destroy your life.** When God told the children of Israel to go into the promised land, He said, "Every place that the sole of your foot shall tread upon, that have I given unto you" (Joshua 1:3). Joshua and Caleb believed that the children of Israel could take the land, but the other spies were afraid of the giants in the land. Because the Israelites listened to the negatives, they wandered in the wilderness of life for 40 long years and died without seeing God's promise fulfilled. If you won't take God at His word and **face** and **fight** your giant head-on, you will wander in the wilderness of life. You will never enter the promised land that God has for you.

We can learn from David — His confidence was in God and God's ability.

I Samuel 17: 34-37; 45-51 Vs. 34 *And David said unto Saul, Thy servant kept his father's sheep, and there came a lion, and a bear, and took a lamb out of the flock:* Vs. 35 *And I went out after him, and smote him, and delivered it out of his mouth: and when he arose against me, I caught him by his beard, and smote him, and slew him.*

Vs. 36 *Thy servant slew both the lion and the bear: and this uncircumcised Philistine shall be as one of them, seeing he hath defied the armies of the living God.* Vs. 37 *David said moreover, The LORD that delivered me out of the paw of the lion, and out of the paw of the bear, he will deliver me out of the hand of this Philistine. And Saul said unto David, Go, and the LORD be with thee.*

Vs. 45 *Then said David to the Philistine, Thou comest to me with a sword, and with a spear, and with a shield: but I come to thee in the name of the LORD of hosts, the God of the armies of Israel, whom thou hast defied.* Vs. 46 *This day will the LORD deliver thee into mine hand; and I will smite thee, and take thine head from thee; and I will give the carcases of the host of the Philistines this day unto the fowls of the air, and to the wild beasts of the earth; that all the earth may know that there is a God in Israel.*

Vs. 47 *And all this assembly shall know that the LORD saveth not with sword and spear: for the battle is the LORD's, and he will give you into our hands.* Vs. 48 *And it came to pass, when the Philistine arose, and came and drew nigh to meet David, that David hasted, and ran toward the army to meet the Philistine.*

Vs. 49 *And David put his hand in his bag, and took thence a stone, and slang it, and smote the Philistine in his forehead, that the stone sunk into his forehead; and he fell upon his face to the earth.* **Vs. 50** *So David prevailed over the Philistine with a sling and with a stone, and smote the Philistine, and slew him; but there was no sword in the hand of David.*

Vs. 51 *Therefore David ran, and stood upon the Philistine, and took his sword, and drew it out of the sheath thereof, and slew him, and cut off his head therewith. And when the Philistines saw their champion was dead, they fled.*

David conquered his *zuzim* and took him out. He did it because he trusted not in his own ability, but in God's ability. You and I can conquer the giants in our lives by realizing that we cannot do it in the flesh—but we can do it by the **power** of **God** and with the **help** of the **Holy Spirit.**

THIRTY-ONE
I AM *that* I AM

Exodus 3:14 *And God said unto Moses, I AM THAT I AM: and he said, Thus shalt thou say unto the children of Israel, I AM hath sent me unto you.*

Genesis 1:1 says that in the beginning, God created everything—God created the heavens and the earth. It all began with Him. So when God tells Moses that "I am that I am" He means just that. He has no one higher than Himself. He is El Shaddai—the all sufficient one—the God of plenty. He is more than enough!

Revelation 1: 4 *John to the seven churches which are in Asia: Grace be unto you, and peace, from him which is, and which was, and which is to come; and from the seven Spirits which are before his throne.*

God is, He was, and He is to come.

Revelation 1:11 *Saying, I am Alpha and Omega, the first and the last: and, What thou seest, write in a book, and send it unto the seven churches which are in Asia; unto Ephesus, and unto Smyrna, and unto Pergamos, and unto Thyatira, and unto Sardis, and unto Philadelphia, and unto Laodicea.*

He is the Alpha and the Omega—the beginning and the end.

Revelation 1:17 *And when I saw him, I fell at his feet as dead. And he laid his right hand upon me, saying unto me, Fear not; I am the first and the last.*

The Lord is the first and the last.

I know this seems too much for the human mind to comprehend, because we have a beginning and we have an ending. We were created. We are subject to the natural realm. We are stuck in the realm of time and space, whereas God is in the realm of the Spirit, a dimension we cannot comprehend with our five physical senses. Before creation, God was. He brought creation into being. How can beings who can only relate to time understand eternity—where time does not exist as they know it?

Our problem is that we are finite beings, trying to understand an infinite God. We know we can trust God and that His Word is true. We know that everything He says about Himself is true. Therefore, we can accept everything He says about Himself and believe it absolutely. Just because we cannot figure it out, and because we cannot explain it in terms we can relate to, does not mean it is not so. We need to get away from the line of thinking and reasoning that if it does not make sense to us, it isn't so. If God says it, it is true! We can accept it because God said it!

God always was and always will be. That is what makes Him God. I AM THAT I AM is all that we need.

THIRTY-TWO
OUR CHRISTIAN CODE *of* CONDUCT

I Peter 2:9-19 (Amp) Vs. 9 *But you are a chosen race, a royal priesthood, a dedicated nation [God's] own purchased, special people, that you may set forth the wonderful deeds and display the virtues and perfections of Him Who called you out of darkness into His marvelous light.* Vs. 10 *Once you were not a people [at all], but now you are God's people; once you were unpitied, but now you are pitied and have received mercy.*

Vs. 11 *Beloved, I implore you as aliens and strangers and exiles [in this world] to abstain from the sensual urges (the evil desires, the passions of the flesh, your lower nature) that wage war against the soul.* Vs. 12 *Conduct yourselves properly (honorably, righteously) among the Gentiles, so that, although they may slander you as evildoers, [yet] they may by witnessing your good deeds [come to] glorify God in the day of inspection [when God shall look upon you wanderers as a pastor or shepherd looks over his flock].*

Vs.13 *Be submissive to every human institution and authority for the sake of the Lord, whether it be to the emperor as supreme,* Vs. 14 *Or to governors as sent by him to bring vengeance (punishment, justice) to those who do wrong and to encourage those who do good service.*

Vs. 15 *For it is God's will and intention that by doing right [your good and honest lives] should silence (muzzle, gag) the ignorant charges and ill-informed criticisms of foolish persons.* Vs. 16 *[Live] as free people, [yet] without employing your freedom as a pretext for wickedness; but [live at all times] as servants of God.*

Vs. 17 *Show respect for all men [treat them honorably]. Love the brotherhood (the Christian fraternity of which Christ is the Head). Reverence God. Honor the emperor.* Vs. 18 *[You who are] household servants, be submissive to your masters with all [proper] respect, not only to those who are kind and considerate and reasonable, but also to those who are surly (overbearing, unjust, and crooked).*

Vs. 19 *For one is regarded favorably (is approved, acceptable, and thankworthy) if, as in the sight of God, he endures the pain of unjust suffering.*

As Christians, we are chosen by God and called out of darkness to set forth His wonderful deeds and display His virtues and perfection. In order to do this, the Lord asks us to conduct ourselves honorably and righteously, especially among unsaved people, so that even though they may criticize us, they ultimately will respect us.

We have been born into a new family, into a new nation. We are like aliens in this world. Our sensual nature, our flesh, which is trained in the ways and desires of the world, wars against our inner man that is full of the nature of God. We have to make the choice to say "no" to our flesh and "yes" to God.

Rebellion in any form is ungodly. Sometimes people use their principles as an excuse for their rebellion. If we are rebellious in the natural, we will almost definitely be rebellious when it comes to spiritual things. The Bible tells us to be submissive to those in authority over us — human institutions and authorities, emperors (presidents) governors, etc. If we disagree with decisions made, we need to go through the proper channels to let our convictions be known. After that, it is up to God — every man will stand accountable to God, not to us as mere men! God does not hold us responsible for other people's actions, either.

We are to submit to our bosses and show them respect, whether they are good and kind or mean and crooked. Their realm of authority over us is the workplace. They do not have authority over our private lives unless it directly affects our job. We are not required to break the law to obey our boss, either—in that case a higher law, the law of the land, would apply. We are free to inform the police of illegal activity.

Under normal circumstances, we need to give our best and do our best on the job so that God can be glorified by our conduct. If the company pays the salary, we must give them our best. If the conditions are so bad that we cannot give our best, we are free to leave. But who knows—perhaps God sent us to that job to be an example of God's love and to lead our boss to the Lord!

We must treat all men honorably and show love to our brothers and sisters in the Lord. Be a person who keeps his word. Be a person of integrity. Show integrity toward your husband or wife. Don't dishonor them. Keep your word to your children. If you are divorced from your spouse, make sure you fulfill your obligations to your children. Always pay what you commit to pay. Always choose the high road. Do the right thing even if it is uncomfortable or if it makes your flesh scream!

It is God's will and plan for us that the criticisms and ignorant charges leveled against us will be silenced by our good and honest lives and conduct. We are free *from* sin and all other bondage, but we are not free to sin or to disobey our Father, God.

THIRTY-THREE
AGREEMENT-*the* KEY TO ANSWERED PRAYER *and* A SUCCESSFUL LIFE

Luke 11:14-23 Vs. 14 *And he was casting out a devil, and it was dumb. And it came to pass, when the devil was gone out, the dumb spake; and the people wondered.* Vs. 15 *But some of them said, He casteth out devils through Beelzebub the chief of the devils.*

Vs. 16 *And others, tempting him, sought of him a sign from heaven.* Vs. 17 *But he, knowing their thoughts, said unto them, Every kingdom divided against itself is brought to desolation; and a house divided against a house falleth.* Vs. 18 *If Satan also be divided against himself, how shall his kingdom stand? Because ye say that I cast out devils through Beelzebub.*

Vs. 19 *And if I by Beelzebub cast out devils, by whom do your sons cast them out? Therefore shall they be your judges.* Vs. 20 *But if I with the finger of God cast out devils, no doubt the kingdom of God is come upon you.* Vs. 21 *When a strong man armed keepeth his palace, his goods are in peace;*

Vs. 22 *But when a stronger than he shall come upon him, and overcome him, he taketh from him all his armour wherein he trusted, and divideth his spoils.* Vs. 23 *He that is not with me is against me: and he that gatheresth not with me scattereth.*

Matthew 18:19, 20 *Again I say unto you, That if two of you shall* *agree on earth as touching any thing that they shall ask, it shall be done for them of my Father which is in heaven. For where two or three are gathered together in my name, there am I in the midst of them.*

Amos 3:3 *Can two walk together, except they be agreed?*

There is no strength in division, but there is strength in agreement. When we oppose one another, whether it be in our homes or our work or our church, we are weak and our defenses are down. Our churches will never be strong or effective in reaching others with the Good News unless we are united in the love of God. If we cannot bring unity into our homes, they will be broken and our children scattered. When we support one another and stand together, united in goal and purpose, we are strong and we achieve the things we set out to do.

When we disagree with someone, most of the time we expect them to change to come into agreement with us, but we need to stay open to the possibility that we may need to change to agree with them! Agreement is not always a case of "we'll do it *my* way!" To walk in agreement, there needs to be clear communication and a willingness to compromise. However, there are some situations where there is never going to be agreement or compromise. We *cannot* agree with the devil or his lies and we *cannot* compromise the Word of God.

If you are in a church you cannot agree with or if you have a pastor you think is doing or saying things wrong, then you need to check your life. Look at yourself in the mirror of the Word to see if you are the one who needs to change. Perhaps you are uncomfortable because your spirit, by the Holy Spirit, is convicting you of sin and unrighteousness. If your heart does not condemn you, then, if you can, communicate in a kind way with the pastor. If you still cannot agree with the church and/or the pastor, then perhaps you should find another church with which you *can* agree. Better to leave than to stir up strife by trying to change things. In that way, you keep your heart from sinning. God will deal with the pastor if he is wrong.

In your own household, there needs to be unity and agreement. If the husband and wife disagree all the time, there will be trouble in that home. The devil knows how to defeat you—he sows seeds of *strife* and *selfishness* in your relationship. You know how to defeat him—you sow seeds of *love* and *unselfishness* in your marriage and family. Some of the major areas of contention between a husband and wife are discipline of children, and finances. Do whatever is needed to come into agreement over the raising of your children or they will divide and conquer you! Stand together and support each other in the realm of financial needs. When couples hit a rough patch, too many times they begin blaming each other instead of coming into agreement over a solution.

Jesus said that when we agree in prayer, our prayers *are answered* by our Father in heaven. When you have a need in your family, stand together on God's Word. Pray in agreement and God *will answer* your prayer. We are stronger when we agree! We can do more when we agree! The devil cannot confuse, divide or defeat us when we choose to agree.

Deuteronomy 32:30 *How should one chase a thousand, and two put ten thousand to flight, except their Rock had sold them, and the Lord had shut them up?*

We can do *anything*—if God is on our side—and we *agree* with *Him*.

THIRTY – FOUR
SPIRITUAL HUNGER

Isaiah 55:1, 2 *Ho, every one that thirsteth, come ye to the waters, and he that hath no money; come ye, buy, and eat; yea, come, buy wine and milk without money and without price. Wherefore do ye spend money for that which is not bread? And your labour for that which satisfieth not? Hearken diligently unto me, and eat ye that which is good, and let your soul delight itself in fatness.*

Matthew 5:6 *Blessed are they which do hunger and thirst after righteousness: for they shall be filled.*

Spiritual hunger is something that must be cultivated in the life of the believer. In the natural, you can train your appetite to desire certain types of food. If you eat junk food all the time, you will crave junk food. If you eat good food, you will desire good food.

The Word of God uses the words *eat, drink, hunger, thirst*. These references are not related to natural food but to spiritual food. The Bible says that the Word of God and the Spirit of God are spiritual meat, bread, milk, water, and wine to us.

I Peter 2:2 *As newborn babes, desire the sincere milk of the word, that ye may grow thereby.*

This scripture speaks of *desire*. You can have fleshly desires or godly desires. You have to turn your heart toward God and His Word and cultivate a desire for the things of God. You need to develop your spiritual appetite so that you can agree with the Psalmist as he wrote in Psalm 42:1 *As the hart* (deer) *panteth after the water brooks, so panteth my soul after thee, O God.*

You can say, "Lord, I am so very hungry and thirsty for You. I need You in my life. You are everything I long for; You are everything I need. I want more of You in my life.

"I want to spend time in Your presence; I want to hide Your Word in my heart, so that I might not sin against You. I don't want to grieve You or upset You. I want to know You more. Every waking moment I am thinking about You and my desire is toward You. I want to know You more and more each day."

The only way you are going to cultivate more of a desire for God's Word is by spending time in His Word, in His presence, and with His people.

THIRTY-FIVE
BEING FAITHFUL *with* THAT *with* WHICH THE LORD *has* BLESSED YOU

Matthew 25:14-23 Vs. 14 *For the kingdom of heaven is as a man travelling into a far country, who called his own servants, and delivered unto them his goods.* Vs. 15 *And unto one he gave five talents, to another two, and to another one; to every man according to his several ability; and straightway took his journey.*

Vs. 16 *Then he that had received the five talents went and traded with the same, and made them other five talents.* Vs. 17 *And likewise he that had received two, he also gained other two.* Vs. 18 *But he that had received one went and digged in the earth, and hid his lord's money.*

Vs. 19 *After a long time the lord of those servants cometh, and reckoneth with them.* Vs. 20 *And so he that had received five talents came and brought other five talents, saying, Lord, thou deliveredst unto me five talents: behold, I have gained beside them five talents more.*

Vs. 21 *His lord said unto him, Well done thou good and faithful servant: thou hast been faithful over a few things, I will make thee ruler over many things: enter thou into the joy of thy lord.* Vs. 22 *He also that had received two talents came and said, Lord, thou deliveredst unto me two talents: behold, I have gained two other talents beside them.*

Vs. 23 *His lord said unto him, Well done, good and faithful servant; thou hast been faithful over a few things, I will make thee ruler over many things: enter thou into the joy of thy lord.*

Many times we tend to look on someone else's talents (that with which the Lord has blessed them) and feel intimidated because we feel that what we have is inferior, insignificant, and of no consequence. This pressure can leave us frustrated and unhappy with what we have, and always striving to get to this imaginary place — living in the Land of Nowhere, trying to get somewhere.

God has blessed each of us (verse 15), and if we are faithful with a little, He makes us ruler over much. I would like to give you some guidelines for your life that I believe will help you remain faithful to what the Lord has blessed you with.

1. Don't look at what others have been blessed with and compare yourself to them.
2. Use your talent, no matter how small — use it or lose it.
3. Be faithful with a little and He will make you a ruler over much.
4. Use the blessings of others as encouragement and inspiration to you.
5. Be happy and rejoice in the little things and praise Him — then watch what God will do in your life.
6. Don't bury your talent, use it — believe God to double it as you are faithful.

THIRTY-SIX
GIVING *as* A LIFESTYLE

Deuteronomy 16:16, 17 (Amp) *Three times a year shall all your males appear before the Lord your God in the place which He chooses: at the Feast of Unleavened Bread, at the Feast of Weeks, and at the Feast of Tabernacles or Booths. They shall not appear before the Lord empty-handed. Every man shall give as he is able, according to the blessing of the Lord your God which He has given you.*

Under the Old Covenant, the presence of God resided in the Ark of the Covenant. God's people would travel to Jerusalem, where the Ark was, to celebrate the feasts that God ordained and to make sacrifices to the Lord, and worship Him there. The Lord also instructed them to bring something with them to give as an offering, every time they came. They were not supposed to come to Jerusalem to worship the Lord empty-handed.

You will notice that God did not ask them to bring what they did not have or to give more than they were capable of giving. All He asked was that they bring something, a portion, of what they had in their possession, according to the blessing of the Lord that was on their lives. It is important to note that God is the One who had blessed them with what they had in the first place. All He asked was a small portion in return. Some people treat God like He is a taker, always taking away from us, begrudging us the little we do have. They think God gives things to us, but then rips them away before we can enjoy them. On the contrary, one of God's greatest desires is to *bless* us.

Deuteronomy 30:8, 9 (Amp) *And you shall return and obey the voice of the Lord and do all His commandments which I command you today. And the Lord your God will make you abundantly prosperous in every work of your hand, in the fruit of your body, of your cattle, of your land, for good; for the Lord will again delight in prospering you, as He took delight in your fathers.*

How wonderful to know that our Father God *delights* in blessing us. He *delights* to bless the work of our hands, our children, and everything we have and own. But He cannot bless us unless we give Him something to work with. God is the all-time biggest giver this universe has ever known. He operates by His own mandate — give and it shall be given back to you! (Luke 6:38) Whatever you sow, you will reap. (Galatians 6:7) God wants us to learn to be givers in every area of our lives — money, possessions, love, forgiveness, kindness — so that He can turn right around and bless us abundantly, according to His Word.

If for no other reason than a desire to be *like* our Father, we should learn to be generous givers, using every opportunity we have to give — being *open-handed* and *open-hearted*! Whatever we do, whenever we give, we should give as if we are giving to the Lord Himself, because He is the source of our blessing. We should give generously according to His blessing that is *already* in our lives. If we obey God in our giving — the cycle of blessing will never end!

THIRTY-SEVEN

HOW to GIVE ACCORDING to the WORD of GOD

If we want to receive the blessings that God promises, we must obey His Word and His commandments. God is a giver, and as His children, we are just like Him—we are givers. God's Word tells us *how* to give. We must give according to God's Word, if we want to receive the blessings that He promises to us. We must give according to God's Word, just because we love Him and want to obey Him.

WE MUST GIVE A GOOD MEASURE

Luke 6:38 *Give, and it shall be given unto you; good measure, pressed down, and shaken together, and running over, shall men give into your bosom. For with the same measure that ye mete withal it shall be measured to you again.*

WE MUST GIVE AS GOD HAS PROSPERED US

I Corinthians 16:2 (Amp) *On the first [day] of each week, let each one of you [personally] put aside something and save it up as he has prospered [in proportion to what he is given], so that no collections will need to be taken after I come.* KJV . . . as God hath prospered him . . .

WE MUST GIVE WILLINGLY

II Corinthians 8:12 (Amp) *For if the [eager] readiness to give is there, then it is acceptable and welcomed in proportion to what a person has, not according to what he does not have.*

WE MUST GIVE GENEROUSLY

II Corinthians 9:6 (Amp) *[Remember] this: he who sows sparingly and grudgingly will also reap sparingly and grudgingly, and he who sows generously [that blessings may come to someone] will also reap generously and with blessings.*

WE MUST GIVE WITH PURPOSE

II Corinthians 9:7a (Amp) *Let each one [give] as he has made up his own mind and purposed in his heart, not reluctantly or sorrowfully or under compulsion . . .*

WE MUST GIVE CHEERFULLY

II Corinthians 9:7b (Amp) *. . . for God loves (He takes pleasure in, prizes above other things, and is unwilling to abandon or to do without) a cheerful (joyous, "prompt to do it") giver [whose heart is in his giving].*

THE BLESSING

II Corinthians 9:8 (Amp) *And God is able to make all grace (every favor and earthly blessing) come to you in abundance, so that you may always and under all circumstances and whatever the need be self-sufficient [possessing enough to require no aid or support and furnished in abundance for every good work and charitable donation].*

THIRTY-EIGHT
THE GLORY *of* GOD

II Chronicles 5:11-14 Vs. 11 *And it came to pass, when the priests were come out of the holy place: (for all the priests that were present were sanctified, and did not then wait by course:* Vs. 12 *Also the Levites which were the singers, all of them of Asaph, of Heman, of Jeduthun, with their sons and their brethren, being arrayed in white linen, having cymbals and psalteries and harps, stood at the east end of the altar, and with them an hundred and twenty priests sounding with trumpets:)*

Vs. 13 *It came even to pass, as the trumpeters and singers were as one, to make one sound to be heard in praising and thanking the LORD; and when they lifted up their voice with the trumpets and cymbals and instruments of music, and praised the LORD, saying, For he is good; for his mercy endureth for ever: that then the house was filled with a cloud, even the house of the LORD;* Vs. 14 *So that the priests could not stand to minister by reason of the cloud: for the glory of the Lord had filled the house of God.*

Under the Old Covenant the glory of God manifested as a cloud. Verse 13 says that the house was filled with a cloud of glory and verse 14 says that the priests could not stand to minister because of the cloud. Another translation says that **the priests could not perform their ministerial duties.** Yet another translation says that **the priests could not function.** It is amazing to think that even under the Old Covenant, God manifested His presence in such an awesome way. Can you imagine what it must have been like to actually see His glory with your eyes?

THE OLD COVENANT
VERSUS *the* NEW COVENANT

II Corinthians 3:7-9 *But if the ministration of death, written and engraven in stones, was glorious, so that the children of Israel could not stedfastly behold the face of Moses for the glory of his countenance; which glory was to be done away: How shall not the ministration of the spirit be rather glorious? For if the ministration of condemnation be glory, much more doth the ministration of righteousness exceed in glory.*

This was referring to the Old Covenant versus the New Covenant, showing that even though the Old was glorious, the New is now greater than the Old in glory.

The exciting thing for us, as believers, is to know that when Jesus cried, "It is finished!" the veil of the temple was torn in two from top to bottom. The Holy Spirit came out of the earthly tabernacle, made with the hands of man, never again to live therein. He now lives in my heart and your heart—we become the temple of the living God.

We have this treasure—the glory of God inside of us—**in earthen vessels.**

II Corinthians 4: 6, 7 *For God, who commanded the light to shine out of darkness, hath shined in our hearts, to give the light of the knowledge of the glory of God in the face of Jesus Christ. But we have this treasure in earthen vessels, that the excellency of the power may be of God, and not of us.*

It is because of the blood of Jesus and the cross of Christ that this has been made possible. Many believers do not realize what took place at Calvary. They do not realize what it was that was purchased for them. Jesus' death and resurrection restored to us the glory of God. The glory of God is God's presence made available to the Church. The glory of God indwells us, sustains us, leads us, protects us, guides us, and quickens us. **To God be the glory.**

THIRTY-NINE
THE PURE *in* HEART SHALL PROSPER

III John 2 (Amp) *Beloved, I pray that you may prosper in every way and [that your body] may keep well, even as [I know] your soul keeps well and prospers.*

There are several Hebrew words for "prosperity" in the Bible. According to the Bible, the word "prosperity" can also be defined as success, wisdom, understanding, health, peace, favor, abundance, quietness, cheerfulness, ease, joyfulness, pleasure, and wealth. Our Father God loves us, His children. He wants to bless us, *spirit, soul and body.* He wants the very best for us just as we, as earthly parents, want the best for our children.

I Corinthians 16:2 *Upon the first day of the week let every one of you lay by him in store, as God hath prospered him, that there be no gatherings when I come.*

God is the One who prospers His people. Religion and tradition have put forth the idea that God is the author and proponent of poverty and that His perfect will for us is poverty. The devil is actually the author of these false teachings. He wants God's people to believe that God does not want them blessed.

Psalm 35:27 (Amp) *Let those who favor my righteous cause and have pleasure in my uprightness shout for joy and be glad and say continually, Let the Lord be magnified, Who takes pleasure in the prosperity of His servant.*

The Lord takes *pleasure* in His children's and servants' prosperity. God is not unhappy when we do well and are blessed – He is happy for us. God does not mind if we *have things* – He does mind if *things have us*. The word "prosperity" is a dirty word in some religious circles, but the truly dirty word should be "covetousness."

Luke 12:15 (Amp) *And He said to them, Guard yourselves and keep free from all covetousness (the immoderate desire for wealth, the greedy longing to have more); for a man's life does not consist in and is not derived from possessing overflowing abundance or that which is over and above his needs.*

Your value as a person is not in the things you have, but in who you *are*. Things – possessions – will not make you happy.

Ephesians 5:5 and Colossians 3:5 both say that covetousness is idolatry. If we worship possessions, we will not have God's blessing – if we worship God, we will have God's blessings.

Deuteronomy 29:9 (Amp) *Therefore keep the words of this covenant and do them, that you may deal wisely and prosper in all that you do.*

Job 36:11 (Amp) *If they obey and serve Him, they shall spend their days in prosperity and their years in pleasantness and joy.*

God's principles work 180 degrees opposite to the world's ideas. The world's wisdom says, "Go after things and you will have them." God says, "Go after Me and you will have the things you need." Covetousness will not bring blessing to your life, only bondage. Serving God with all your heart will bring you all the blessing you can handle. Put your heart on the things of God and you will have His prosperity.

FORTY
THE RESTORER *of* WASTED YEARS

Joel 2:23-25 Vs. 23 *Be glad then, ye children of Zion, and rejoice in the Lord your God: for he hath given you the former rain moderately, and he will cause to come down for you the rain, the former rain, and the latter rain in the first month.*

Vs. 24 *And the floors shall be full of wheat, and the vats shall overflow with wine and oil.* Vs. 25 *And I will restore to you the years that the locust hath eaten, the cankerworm, and the caterpillar, and the palmerworm, my great army which I sent among you.*

When people come to know God for the first time—especially when they come to Him in later life—it may feel like they have wasted so many years. They may feel that there is no way they can have those years restored. Those are the lost years of an individual's life. But Joel 2:25 says that **God will restore to you the years that the locusts have eaten.**

I think of the prodigal son and how he spent all his inheritance on riotous living. (Luke 15:11-24) He ended up in the pigpen of life. He was so low that even the pigpen and pig slop started to look good.

The Bible says that he came to his senses and said to himself, "I will arise and go to my father, and will say unto him, 'Father, I have sinned against heaven and before thee, and am no more worthy to be called thy son. Make me as one of thy hired servants.'"

The Word says that the father saw him a long way off and ran to greet him. He kissed him, put a ring on his finger, put a robe on his back and killed the fatted calf for him. **The Father restored the years that the locusts had eaten** and gave him back his place in the family.

It doesn't matter where you come from or what you have done. Whether you come to God for the very first time or if you are the prodigal child come back to God in repentance, He always restores to you that which the enemy has stolen. He is the restorer of your wasted years.

FORTY-ONE

THE COMMUNION of the BLOOD and BODY of CHRIST

1 Corinthians 10:16-22 Vs. 16 *The cup of blessing which we bless, is it not the communion of the blood of Christ? The bread which we break, is it not the communion of the body of Christ? Vs. 17 For we being many are one bread, and one body; for we are all partakers of that one bread.*

Vs. 18 *Behold Israel after the flesh: are not they which eat of the sacrifices partakers of the altar?* Vs. 19 *What say I then? That the idol is any thing, or that which is offered in sacrifice to idols is any thing?*

Vs. 20 *But I say, that the things which the Gentiles sacrifice, they sacrifice to devils, and not to God: and I would not that ye should have fellowship with devils.* Vs. 21 *Ye cannot drink the cup of the Lord, and the cup of devils: ye cannot be partakers of the Lord's table, and of the table of devils.* Vs. 22 *Do we provoke the Lord to jealousy? Are we stronger than he?*

When we come to the table of the Lord, we come to the table of the covenant. We remember His death, burial and resurrection until He comes. *This is my Body that was broken for you-this is my Blood that was shed for you.* This is a living meal that speaks of the finished work of the cross of Calvary.

We show our commitment to the Lord in our communion

with Him, also by pledging our allegiance to Him. This commitment is to Christ and to Christ alone. This means that we have no other gods before Him and we are sold out to Him. If we give ourselves 100 percent to the Lord, how can we have communion with the world and the ways of the world and say that we belong to the Lord wholly? We cannot mix the two.

You cannot drink the cup of the Lord and the cup of devils at the same time; you cannot eat at the table of the Lord and the table of devils at the same time. Do we want to provoke the Lord to jealousy or do we want the Lord to know that our communion is with Him and Him alone?

II Corinthians 6:14-18 Vs. 14 *Be ye not unequally yoked together with unbelievers: for what fellowship hath righteousness with unrighteousness? And what communion hath light with darkness?* Vs. 15 *And what concord hath Christ with Belial? Or what part hath he that believeth with an infidel?*

Vs. 16 *And what agreement hath the temple of God with idols? For ye are the temple of the living God; as God hath said, I will dwell in them, and walk in them; and I will be their God, and they shall be my people.* Vs. 17 *Wherefore come out from among them, and be ye separate, saith the Lord, and touch not the unclean thing; and I will receive you.* Vs. 18 *And will be a Father unto you, and ye shall be my sons and daughters, saith the Lord Almighty.*

Living a holy life consecrated, separated, and yielded to the Lord brings glory to God and does not compromise the table of the Lord.

FORTY-TWO
METHODS and the ANOINTING

John 21:25 *And there are also many other things which Jesus did, the which, if they should be written every one, I suppose that even the world itself could not contain the books that should be written. Amen*

In order to talk about methods and the anointing, we must look at the ministry of Jesus through the eyes of a Pharisee. That might be an easy thing for some of you reading this, and for others it will be hard. Nevertheless, I would like to look at the ministry of Jesus and see if His methods would be acceptable in the day in which we live.

I am positive that if Jesus were here today in the flesh, He would be kicked out of most churches and would not be invited to speak at most conferences. Why? Because of HIS METHODS. If His methods were put under scrutiny, many would not receive Him today, just as they did not receive Him yesterday. Let's look at some of the methods He used that would cause a problem today.

1. He was constantly with sinners and publicans and was accused of being a gluttonous man, a wine bibber.
2. He healed on the Sabbath Day.
3. His disciples did not wash their hands when they ate.
4. His disciples did not keep the traditions of the elders.
5. They ate on the Sabbath.
6. He walked on water.

7. He went over to the country of the Gadarenes and caused havoc by casting devils out of the man bound with a legion—this resulted in a whole herd of swine running down a hill into the sea and drowning. The people then begged him to leave their country.
8. When they needed tax money, He told them to go fishing and take the coins out of the fishes' mouths.
9. He stopped a funeral procession and raised the boy from the dead.
10. He spat in the ground and made clay, then put it on a man's eyes and told him to go wash in the Pool of Siloam.
11. He called the Syrophoenecian woman a dog.
12. He got angry and cursed a fig tree.
13. He lost His temper when He went into the temple, and overturned the tables of the moneychangers, then beat them with whips.
14. Some of His meetings were out of order because the roof was ripped off a house and a man was let down through the hole in the roof.
15. Made strong statements like "Unless you eat of my flesh and drink of my blood..."
16. When some people wanted to follow Him but remarked that they wanted to go home and bury their father, He said, "Let the dead bury the dead."
17. Stood by the offering and watched it being received, and called His disciples to come and observe.
18. Allowed people to go walking and leaping and praising God in His services.
19. Allowed a woman to pour expensive perfume on His head when the money could have been given to the poor.
20. Did not show up to attend a dear friend's funeral—Lazarus—and waited four days until He raised him from the dead.
21. Called people "blind leading the blind"—"whitewashed sepulchres of dead men's of vipers"—"you are of your

father the devil."
22. Had unclean spirits cry out with loud voices in the synagogue.
23. Let a woman caught in adultery go when she should have been stoned.
24. Offended a rich young ruler by telling him that he had to sell all and give to the poor.
25. Healed a man, then forgave him of his sin—he said that both were easy.
26. When He called people, He had no communication with them about their past life—He accepted them just as they were.
27. He breathed on His disciples and said, "Receive ye the Holy Ghost."

FORTY-THREE

THE POWER of FORGIVENESS

Mark 11:22-26 (Amp) Vs. 22 *And Jesus, replying, said to them, Have faith in God [constantly]. Vs. 23 Truly I tell you, whoever says to this mountain, Be lifted up and thrown into the sea! and does not doubt at all in his heart but believes that what he says will take place, it will be done for him.*

Vs. 24 For this reason I am telling you, whatever you ask for in prayer, believe (trust and be confident) that it is granted to you, and you will [get it]. Vs. 25 And whenever you stand praying, if you have anything against anyone, forgive him and let it drop (leave it, let it go), in order that your Father Who is in heaven may also forgive you your [own] failings and shortcomings and let them drop. Vs. 26 But if you do not forgive, neither will your Father in heaven forgive your failings and shortcomings.

Our prayers and our faith will not work if we are carrying unforgiveness toward others in our hearts. We must forgive others before we can expect any results from our prayers to the Father. Sin separates us from the presence of God and unforgiveness is sin. 1 Corinthians 13:2 (Amp) says that I can have sufficient faith to remove mountains, but if I do not have love, I am nothing — a useless nobody.

Isaiah 43:25 (Amp) *I, even I, am He Who blots out and cancels your transgressions, for My own sake, and I will not remember your sins.*

Psalm 103:12 (Amp) *As far as the east is from the west, so far has He removed our transgressions from us.*

The Father wipes our slate completely clean. He blots out our sins, removing them as far as possible from us, and He even chooses to forget them! When we forgive others, part of the process is to forget. If we continually remind ourselves of the wrong we suffered, we have not truly forgiven the person who offended us. Forgive and forget. Forgive and let it go.

Matthew 18:21, 22 (Amp) *Then Peter came up to Him and said, Lord, how many times may my brother sin against me and I forgive him and let it go? [As many as] up to seven times? Jesus answered him, I tell you, not up to seven times, but seventy times seven!*

We are to forgive over and over and over again. We have a tendency to think we need to forgive only once—and then judgment comes. If the person transgresses again, they receive no more mercy from us. However, the Father wants us to forgive all the time—time after time.

Matthew 18:23-35 is the parable of the king who wished to settle the accounts of his servants. He had a servant who owed him 10,000 talents—about $10,000,000. Because the servant could not pay, the king ordered him, his wife, his children, and his possessions to be sold to settle the debt. The servant begged for patience, promising to pay, and his master had compassion on him and canceled the debt. However, that same servant went out and threw a fellow servant into prison because he owed him 100 denarii—about $20! When the king heard of his bad attitude, he had the servant thrown into jail and ordered him to pay the original debt. Verse 35 (Amp) says, *So also My heavenly*

Father will deal with every one of you if you do not freely forgive your brother from your heart his offenses.

If we want to experience the Father's forgiveness and mercy in our lives, we should truly forgive others and have mercy on them.

FORTY-FOUR
HEALING - IS *it* GOD'S WILL?

Exodus 15:26 . . . *If thou wilt diligently hearken to the voice of the Lord thy God, and wilt do that which is right in his sight, and wilt give ear to his commandments and keep all his statutes, I will put none of these diseases upon thee, which I have brought upon the Egyptians: for I am the Lord that healeth thee.*

One of the main arguments in the religious world among theologians is — **is healing God's will or not?** A problem arises because many people do not understand the character of God and how He loves us. They say that God places sickness on people to teach them a lesson and yet these same afflicted people go to doctors and take medication trying to get healed from what God, supposedly, has put on them. Twenty years later they seem not to have learned the lesson that God apparently wanted to teach them. In the scripture above, God says, "I will put none of these diseases on you." In light of other scriptures, the word "put" should be rendered more like "permit."

The Bible is clear on the fact that sickness does not originate from God and is not in His character. God *allowed* them to be smitten because of their sin. God is not a robber and a thief; He is a good God Who loves us very much. He not only wants to save us, but also to heal us.

It is God's nature and character to heal and bless. It is important for every believer to settle in his own heart once and for all that the nature and character of God is to save, heal, and deliver. The nature of the devil is to kill, steal, and destroy. The full character of God can be seen through the ministry of Jesus Christ.

Mark 1:39-42 Vs. 39 *And he preached in their synagogues throughout all Galilee, and cast out devils.* Vs. 40 *And there came a leper to him, beseeching him, and kneeling down to him, and saying unto him, If thou wilt, thou canst make me clean.* Vs. 41 *And Jesus, moved with compassion, put forth his hand, and touched him, and saith unto him, I will; be thou clean.* Vs. 42 *And as soon as he had spoken, immediately the leprosy departed from him, and he was cleansed.*

He said to the leper, "I will—be thou cleansed." He said that He did not come to do His own will but "the will of Him that sent Me."

In Mark 2:1-13, Jesus said that it was as easy to forgive sin as it is to heal. In other words, he put sickness and sin in the same category. Read this passage of scripture in your personal study, and notice especially verses 9 through 11: Vs. 9 *Whether is it easier to say to the sick of the palsy, Thy sins be forgiven thee; or to say, Arise, and take up thy bed, and walk?* Vs. 10 *But that ye may know that the Son of man hath power on earth to forgive sins, (he saith to the sick of the palsy,)* Vs. 11 *I say unto thee, Arise, and take up thy bed, and go thy way into thine house.*

This is so plain—I don't know why God's people cannot see it. It seems to me that there must be a reading problem in the church—because it is plain, even for this African boy, to see.

Acts 10:38 *How God anointed Jesus of Nazareth with the Holy Ghost and with power: who went about **doing good**, and **healing all** that were **oppressed of the devil**; for God was with him.*

The devil is the oppressor but God is the Healer. In Exodus 23:25, God's Word says, *And ye shall serve the Lord your God, and he shall bless thy bread, and thy water; and I will take sickness away from the midst of thee.*

God gives us a choice—because Jesus paid the price for sickness and sin on the cross 2,000 years ago. Salvation and healing go hand in hand.

The choice is ours—**Deuteronomy 30:19** *I call heaven and earth to record this day against you, that I have set before you life and death, blessing and cursing: **therefore choose life,** that both thou and thy seed may live.*

The choice is yours. *"I am the God that healeth thee."* It is God's will to heal you, just as it is His will to save you. Settle that for yourself once and for all.

FORTY-FIVE
FAITH'S DEFINITIONS

Hebrews 10:38-39 Vs. 38 *Now the just shall live by faith: but if any man draw back, my soul shall have no pleasure in him.* Vs. 39 *But we are not of them who draw back unto perdition; but of them that believe to the saving of the soul.*

It is evident as we read the Word of God that faith is one of the main pillars in our walk with God; a thorough study of the whole of Hebrews 11, the "Hall of Faith," will reveal this. As we go into Hebrews 12, we see that Jesus is the author and finisher of our faith. Faith **has been used as though it were a formula, but faith is simply God's children trusting in God's Word, His promises, and His ability.**

Hebrews 11:6 *But without faith it is impossible to please him: for he that cometh to God must believe that he is, and that he is a rewarder of them that diligently seek him.*

Everything you and I receive from God is a result of trusting Him and His Word.

Faith is believing in the integrity of the One who promised. Faith is acting upon God's Word. Faith is grasping the unrealities of hope and bringing them into the realm of reality. Faith is the title deed of things (hoped) prayed for.

Faith counts it done, without any other proof in the natural than God's Word (no experience or feeling).

Faith has nothing to do with your five senses.

Faith has a voice and it speaks God's Word.

Faith is a spiritual force.

Faith is a confession.

Faith is being fully persuaded.

Faith is a trust in God.

Faith is a guarantee.

DIFFERENT KINDS OF FAITH

1. Great Faith - Matt. 8:10 - 28
2. Weak Faith - Rom.14:1
3. Little Faith - Luke 12:28
4. Saving Faith - Eph. 2:8
5. Healing Faith - Mark 10:52
6. Dead Faith - James 2:17, 26
7. Strong Faith - Rom. 4:20, 21
8. Rich Faith - James 2:5
9. Mustard Seed Faith - Matt.17: 20
10. Overcoming Faith - 1 John 5:4
11. Growing Faith - II Thess. 1:3
12. Creative Faith - Heb. 11:3
13. Praying Faith - James 5:14, 15
14. Tried Faith - 1 Peter 1:7
15. Measure of Faith - Rom. 12:3
16. Justifying Faith - Rom. 5:1
17. Perfect Faith - James 2:22
18. Word of Faith - Rom. 10:8
19. Purifying Faith - Acts 15:8, 9
20. Sanctifying Faith - Acts 26:18
21. Spirit of Faith - II Cor. 4:13
22. Walk of Faith - II Cor. 5:7

23. Shield of Faith - Eph. 6:16
24. Breastplate of Faith - 1 Thess. 5:8
25. Unity of Faith - Eph. 4:13
26. Steadfast Faith - Col. 2:5
27. Gift of Faith - I Cor. 12:9
28. Unfeigned Faith - II Tim.1:5
29. No Faith - Matt. 4:40
30. Visible Faith - Matt.9:2
31. Unfailing Faith - Luke 22:32
32. Full of Faith - Acts 6:5
33. Door of Faith - Acts 14:27
34. Faith that is spoken about - Rom.1:8
35. Mutual Faith - Rom. 1:12
36. Faith to Faith - Rom. 1:17
37. Living by Faith - Rom. 1:17
38. Law of Faith - Rom. 3:27
39. Faith that gives one access - Rom. 5:2
40. Speaking Faith - Rom. 10:6
41. Standing Faith - Rom. 11:20
42. House of Faith - Gal. 6:10
43. One Faith - Eph. 4:5
44. Grounded Faith - Col.1:23
45. Work of Faith - 1 Thess. 1:3
46. First Faith - 1 Tim. 5:12
47. Fight of Faith - II Tim.1:5
48. Keeping Faith - II Tim. 4:7
49. Common Faith - Titus 1:4
50. Sound Faith - Titus 2:2
51. Effectual Faith - Phil. 1:6
52. Rich Faith - James 2:12
53. Precious Faith - II Pet.1:1
54. Holy Faith - Jude 20

FORTY-SIX
TITHES *and* OFFERINGS

Genesis 14:20 *And blessed be the most high God, which hath delivered thine enemies into thy hand. And he gave him tithes of all.*

Hebrews 7:1, 2 Vs. 1 *For this Melchisedec, king of Salem, priest of the most high God, who met Abraham returning from the slaughter of the kings, and blessed him;* Vs. 2 *To whom also Abraham gave a tenth part of all; first being by interpretation King of righteousness, and after that also King of Salem, which is, King of peace;*

Some argue that **tithe** is outdated under the New Covenant because tithing was "under the law." It is interesting to note that Abraham paid tithe before the law ever came into existence, as these two passages reveal. **A tithe is one-tenth of your gross income. An offering is over and above the tithe.**

Malachi 3:8 *Will a man rob God? Yet ye have robbed me. But ye say, Wherein have we robbed thee? In tithes and offerings.*

In this scripture we read about people robbing God because they don't bring their tithe and offerings. The "tithe" is comprised of firstfruits and by bringing the firstfruits, we honor God. We also honor Him by putting His house above our own.

Malachi 3:9 *Ye are cursed with a curse: for ye have robbed me, even this whole nation.*

It is frightening to think that we can rob God, but we can, and robbing Him brings a curse. The moment we don't tithe, we open the door of our lives to the devourer who then comes and steals from us.

Malachi 3:10 *Bring ye all the tithes into the storehouse, that there may be meat in mine house, and prove me now herewith, saith the LORD of hosts, if I will not open you the windows of heaven, and pour you out a blessing, that there shall not be room enough to receive it.*

Bring all the tithe, that there may be meat in mine house, and prove me now herewith...When we "prove" God, we put Him to the test and see that He *will* open the windows of heaven and pour out great blessings upon us. In Hebrew, the word *windows* used in Malachi is the same word used in Genesis to refer to the floodgates. God is saying that He will open the floodgates of heaven and pour out such a blessing on you that there is not enough room to receive it.

Malachi 3:11 *And I will rebuke the devourer for your sakes, and he shall not destroy the fruits of your ground; neither shall your vine cast her fruit before the time in the field, saith the LORD of hosts.*

God says that He will rebuke the devourer so that he shall not destroy the fruits of your ground; when God rebukes the devourer, *he has been rebuked.*

Malachi 3:12 *And all nations shall call you blessed: for ye shall be a delightsome land, saith the LORD of hosts.*

It is the promise of God that all nations shall call you blessed, for you will be blessed. There are many people with financial battles who truly wonder why they never prosper. The reason is simple: they don't tithe. Even if they did tithe at one time, they did it grudgingly. If you have not been tithing, make your decision today to start, then watch the blessing of the Lord begin to unfold in your life. Once you have committed to tithe, extend your faith and begin to sow offerings into the work of the ministry. You will see the windows of heaven open and the blessings come upon you and your storehouses.

FORTY-SEVEN
THE LORD *is* BUILDING *the* HOUSE

Our commission from God when we started the church in Tampa was to "love the people, feed the people, and touch the people" — and it has not changed. Our hearts' desire still is to have a place where people can come and experience the love of God and the power of God, free from the manipulation or control of man.

Psalm 127:1 *Except the Lord build the house, they labour in vain that build it: except the Lord keep the city, the watchman waketh but in vain.*

It is so easy for people to be distracted from what God has for them if they take their eyes off His plan and purpose for their lives, and start looking at what other people are doing or what other people expect. We have to keep our eyes on God's plan for us as pastors, as a church, and as the members of the body.

If God builds the house, then God *must build* the house. He chooses the building material, He decides where everything must go. He decides how big or how small, how many rooms, and the color of the paint. If God truly builds the house, then we need His Word on every detail. He will not give us the commission to build and then leave us to our own devices. He will lead us, guide us, and instruct us every step of the way.

Every one of us has a part to play. Every one of us has something to contribute to the body of Christ in general, and to our local body in particular. We may not currently be aware of our part or what the Lord would have us to do, but we will all find our places as we put God and His Word first place in our lives, and as we grow in grace.

Proverbs 3:1-8 Vs.1 *My son, forget not my law; but let thine heart keep my commandments:* Vs. 2 *For length of days, and long life, and peace, shall they add to thee.* Vs. 3 *Let not mercy and truth forsake thee: bind them about thy neck; write them upon the table of thine heart:* Vs. 4 *So shalt thou find favour and good understanding in the sight of God and man.*

Vs. 5 *Trust in the Lord with all thine heart; and lean not unto thine own understanding.* Vs. 6 *In all thy ways acknowledge him, and he shall direct thy paths.* Vs. 7 *Be not wise in thine own eyes: fear the Lord, and depart from evil.* Vs. 8 *It shall be health to thy navel, and marrow to thy bones.*

John 16:13 *Howbeit when he, the Spirit of truth, is come, he will guide you into all truth: for he shall not speak of himself; but whatsoever he shall hear, that shall he speak: and he will show you things to come.*

The Holy Spirit is our teacher and guide—we cannot follow man. We need to do what the Lord is telling *us, today*. It is a *new* day. God is doing a *new* thing. We need to follow Him. We need to continue to allow the Holy Spirit to lead us, and not allow the enemy or other people's expectations to lead us away from our purpose and call as a church and a revival center. We need to stay hungry for God and keep our eyes on the prize.

FORTY-EIGHT
THE BLESSING *of* THE LORD

Proverbs 10:22 *The blessing of the LORD, it maketh rich, and he addeth no sorrow with it.*

Proverbs 11:10, 11 Vs. 10 *When it goeth well with the righteous, the city rejoiceth: and when the wicked perish, there is shouting.* Vs. 11 *By the blessing of the upright the city is exalted: but it is overthrown by the mouth of the wicked.*

We have "seasons" when we bless others. The Christmas season is a festive time when families get together and bless one another with gifts. It is amazing how just after Thanksgiving, everyone gets into a "blessing" mode which lasts until the day after Christmas. Then it seems like it all comes to an end until the next year.

Some people only bless when it is a loved one's birthday or an anniversary, yet the Lord blesses us every day with His goodness, mercy, and grace. God has a plan and a purpose for your life. When you greet someone and say, "God bless you," you are saying to that person, "God empowers you to prosper." **Jeremiah 29:11** *For I know the thoughts that I think toward you, saith the LORD, thoughts of peace, and not of evil, to give you an expected end.*

God wants to bless you every day of your life, not just once a year. **Psalm 68:19** *Blessed be the Lord, who daily loadeth us with benefits, even the God of our salvation.* The Word of God declares that the blessing of the Lord makes one rich and He adds no sorrow with it. The blessing of the world has a sting in the tail. Worldly pursuits, without God, promise pleasure, but deliver destruction. You may have every advantage in this world, money, position, and influence, but if you die without Jesus—earth will be the only heaven you ever know. Even with the current rate of inflation, the wages of sin is still death.

David said in **Psalm 37:25** *I have been young, and now am old; yet have I not seen the righteous forsaken, nor his seed begging bread.* Why could he say this? Because he had seen firsthand God's blessing in his life. He wrote **Psalm 23:**

Vs. 1 *The LORD is my shepherd; I shall not want.* Vs. 2 *He maketh me to lie down in green pastures: he leadeth me beside the still waters.* Vs. 3 *He restoreth my soul: he leadeth me in the paths of righteousness for his name's sake.*

Vs. 4 *Yea, though I walk through the valley of the shadow of death, I will fear no evil: for thou art with me; thy rod and thy staff they comfort me.* Vs. 5 *Thou preparest a table before me in the presence of mine enemies: thou anointest my head with oil; my cup runneth over.* Vs. 6 *Surely goodness and mercy shall follow me all the days of my life: and I will dwell in the house of the LORD for ever.*

Psalm 84:10-12 Vs. 10 *For a day in thy courts is better than a thousand. I had rather be a doorkeeper in the house of my God, than to dwell in the tents of wickedness.* Vs. 11 *For the LORD God is a sun and shield: the LORD will give grace and glory: no good thing will he withhold from them that walk uprightly.* Vs. 12 *O LORD of hosts, blessed is the man that trusteth in thee.*

There is nothing like the blessing of the Lord. I remember the time when we were not yet walking in the blessing that was purchased at Calvary's cross through the blood of Jesus Christ. I also remember what it was like when we first began to walk in His blessing. I'm telling you, we had to pinch ourselves because we thought we had died and gone to heaven. It is awesome! I would not change it for anything the world has to offer. God's blessing is upon me and because His blessing is upon me, I can bless others.

FORTY-NINE
GLAD TIDINGS *of* GREAT JOY

Luke 2:8-14 *Vs. 8 And there were in the same country shepherds abiding in the field, keeping watch over their flock by night. Vs. 9 And, lo, the angel of the Lord came upon them, and the glory of the Lord shone round about them: and they were sore afraid. Vs. 10 And the angel said unto them, Fear not: for, behold, I bring you good tidings of great joy, which shall be to all people.*

Vs. 11 For unto you is born this day in the city of David a Saviour, which is Christ the Lord. Vs. 12 And this shall be a sign unto you; Ye shall find the babe wrapped in swaddling clothes, lying in a manger. Vs. 13 And suddenly there was with the angel a multitude of the heavenly host praising God, and saying, Vs. 14 Glory to God in the highest, and on earth peace, good will toward men.

The announcement of Jesus' coming was an announcement of joy to the whole world. **"I bring you glad tidings of great joy,"** the angels declared. This was the beginning of **the gospel—the Good News—**being made manifest. Jesus had come, but it was not the *baby* Jesus that was going to do the work. That baby was going to grow up and fulfill the purpose for which He was born.

I John 3:8 *He that committeth sin is of the devil; for the devil sinneth from the beginning.* ***For this purpose the Son of God was manifested, that he might destroy the works of the devil.***

Jesus was born to die for mankind, to pay the price for the sin of man. During the Christmas season the world looks toward the birth of the baby Jesus, but they miss the whole point of His coming. He was the Lamb slain before the foundation of the world. As long as you stay around the manger, you can never be born again. As long as you stay around the manger, you can never walk in what was purchased at Calvary's tree. The world needs to realize that the baby in the manger was not the final reason for the glad tiding of great joy. The crucified Lamb—the resurrected Lord Jesus—is our reason for rejoicing. But it just doesn't stop there. He is also seated at the right hand of the Father and He makes intercession for us.

Hebrews 4:14-16 Vs. 14 *Seeing then that we have a great high priest, that is passed into the heavens, Jesus the Son of God, let us hold fast our profession.* Vs. 15 *For we have not an high priest which cannot be touched with the feeling of our infirmities; but was in all points tempted like as we are, yet without sin.* Vs. 16 *Let us therefore come boldly unto the throne of grace, that we may obtain mercy, and find grace to help in time of need.*

The Great High Priest Jesus is the Christ of the empty tomb, the empty cross, and the occupied throne. The glad tidings are that we can walk in the completion of what took place at the Cross of Calvary. During His earthly ministry, Jesus **preached** the glad tidings, He **did** the glad tidings, He **was** the glad tidings.

Luke 4:18,19 Vs. 18 *The Spirit of the Lord is upon me, because he hath anointed me to preach the gospel (Good News) to the poor; he hath sent me to heal the brokenhearted, to preach deliverance to the captives, and recovering of sight to the blind, to set at liberty them that are bruised.* Vs. 19 *To preach the acceptable year of the Lord.*

The acceptable year of the Lord is the Year of Jubilee. The Year of Jubilee represents those wonderful days when salvation and the free favors of God profusely abound. Jesus is our good news, our joy, and our "glad tidings."

FIFTY
ALL THESE THINGS *did* JESUS DO

John 21:25 *And there are also many other things which Jesus did, the which, if they should be written every one, I suppose that even the world itself could not contain the books that should be written. Amen.*

When Jesus walked the earth 2000 years ago, He did not begin His earthly ministry until He was baptized by John in the River Jordan.

Acts 10:38 *How God anointed Jesus of Nazareth with the Holy Ghost and with power: who went about doing good, and healing all that were oppressed of the devil; for God was with him.*

From the time He was anointed to stand in the place of ministry, Jesus began to perform miracles, signs, and wonders. The Word of God declares in John 21:25 that Jesus did so many things (signs, wonders, miracles) that the books of the world could not contain all of them. Jesus performed miracles morning, noon and night.

When I consider what John says, I learn something about Jesus — His ability is limitless. When we get to heaven, I am going to ask the Lord to please show me a replay of His earthly ministry, so that I can fill in the blanks and see and know the things He did that were not written as a record for us on earth.

Now Jesus said, "These works shall ye do and greater works than these shall ye do." This means (in theory, at least, or as far as God is concerned) that the limitless ability that Jesus had is available to us. **"These works"** are the works that Jesus made manifest in Matthew, Mark, Luke and John. Then He added, "**greater works** than these shall ye do." The greater works are now available to us.

A minister told me once, "The greater work is salvation and that is all we are to do—get people saved." I replied, "If that is true, then that is fine with me, because for a person to be born again is surely an incredible miracle; but Jesus also said that **these** works—from Matthew, Mark, Luke, and John—shall ye do." The people who spend the most time arguing about what the **greater** works are, are usually the people who have never even done one of **these** works!

Jesus is living on the inside of you and me, and the Word of God declares that "greater is He that is in you, than he that is in the world." He is on the inside of us so that where we go, Jesus goes. We **can** do the works of Jesus because it is **His ability** that does the work, not ours. We **must** do the works of Jesus because **He tells us** to do them. The more we obey God and the more He can trust us, the more of His anointing He will entrust to us. The more of His anointing we have, the more we will do the works—and the greater works—of Jesus.

FIFTY-ONE
KING *of* KINGS *and* LORD *of* LORDS

Revelation 19:11-16 (Amp) Vs. 11 *After that I saw heaven opened, and behold, a white horse [appeared]! The One Who was riding it is called Faithful (Trustworthy, Loyal, Incorruptible, Steady) and True, and He passes judgment and wages war in righteousness (holiness, justice, and uprightness).* Vs. 12 *His eyes [blaze] like a flame of fire, and on His head are many kingly crowns (diadems); and He has a title (name) inscribed which He alone knows or can understand.*

Vs.13 *He is dressed in a robe dyed by dipping in blood, and the title by which he is called is The Word of God.* Vs. 14 *And the troops of heaven, clothed in fine linen, dazzling and clean, followed Him on white horses.*

Vs. 15 *From His mouth goes forth a sharp sword with which He can smite (afflict, strike) the nations; and He will shepherd and control them with a staff (scepter, rod) of iron. He will tread the winepress of the fierceness of the wrath and indignation of God the All-Ruler (the Almighty, the Omnipotent).* Vs. 16 *And on His garment (robe) and on His thigh He has a name (title) inscribed,* KING OF KINGS AND LORD OF LORDS.

Most of the time when people draw pictures of Jesus, they draw Him as He was in His earthly ministry or on the cross. Even then, the way Jesus is portrayed is not accurate, because we do not know exactly what He looked like. Perhaps artists attempt to portray Jesus' humility or His compassion in some of their works, but many times He comes across looking like a weak and pathetic man.

If you spend any time in the Gospels, with a heart and mind uncluttered by religion, you will read of an incredibly strong individual. Jesus was not concerned with man's opinion of Him. He was brave and honest enough to speak only the truth, even if it offended others. He was courageous enough to go to the cross and unselfishly endure the pain, the suffering, and the humiliation that was our portion.

He did not look pretty on the cross, with only a few small trickles of blood on His head, His hands, His feet, and His side. The Bible says in Isaiah 52:14 (Amp) that He became an object of horror and that His face and appearance was marred more than any man's. He had been so beaten and abused that He was unrecognizable as a person. It was not a pretty sight, but it was done for you and me.

Pictures tend to stay in our minds even if they are not accurate. We need to get a new picture of Jesus in our minds, the picture that the Word of God paints. We need to read the Gospels and see Him as He walked on the earth, for He is our example. We need to know what He went through on the cross, for it is our salvation. However, we also need to know Him as He is now. We need to see Him through the eyes of John, in the Book of Revelation, as he describes to us our *King of kings and Lord of lords!*

He is our *conquering King,* just waiting to return for His own! He has already defeated death, hell, and the grave, and has given to us the keys to the kingdom—the keys to our victory! Let us recognize our *victorious King* and realize that we reign over the devil and life's circumstances together with Him in the authority He has given to us.

Philippians 2:9-11 (Amp) Vs. 9 *Therefore [because He stooped so low] God has highly exalted Him and has freely bestowed on*

Him the name that is above every name. **Vs. 10** *That in (at) the name of Jesus every knee should (must) bow, in heaven and on earth and under the earth,* **Vs. 11** *And every tongue [frankly and openly] confess and acknowledge that Jesus Christ is Lord, to the glory of God the Father.*

Every knee shall bow to the King of kings and every tongue shall and must confess that He is Lord of lords.

Even King Nebuchadnezzar declared that Daniel's God was a God of gods and a Lord of kings. (Daniel 2:46, 47)

Even devils fear and tremble and must declare that Jesus is King and Lord. (James 2:19) If you bow your knee in worship to anyone or anything on this earth, beside God, you are bowing your knee to someone or something that must also bow in worship unto the *King of kings and the Lord of lords.*

FIFTY-TWO
THE POWER *in* YOUR WORDS

Proverbs 18:20, 21 (Amp) Vs. 20 *A man's [moral] self shall be filled with the fruit of his mouth; and with the consequence of his words he must be satisfied [whether good or evil].* Vs. 21 *Death and life are in the power of the tongue, and they who indulge in it shall eat the fruit of it [for death or life].*

You may have heard the saying, "Your life is in your hands." In the Word, the Lord says that your life is in your words. This means that the condition of your life depends upon your words. There are choices you make every day about your life and you are making them with your mouth.

You could be speaking good words over your life or bad words. Perhaps you have reaped a harvest that you do not like, because you have been speaking negative words over yourself. Most of the words we speak are a result of habit. Many times we speak without thinking about what we are saying.

We are so accustomed to saying things a certain way that we do not notice when our words are negative and producing death in our lives. You may have wondered why you seem to always be eating bad fruit, but you may not have connected it to the words you have been speaking for years.

The words you speak carry consequences and you must be satisfied with your harvest. If we were asked what harvest we would like to reap, we would reply that we want a good harvest, a life harvest — not a death harvest. No one in his right mind really wants to reap death and destruction, but that is what we may be reaping as a result of our own words.

Matthew 12:33-37 (Amp) Vs. 33 *Either make the tree sound (healthy and good), and its fruit sound (healthy and good), or make the tree rotten (diseased and bad), and its fruit rotten (diseased and bad); for the tree is known and recognized and judged by its fruit.*

Vs. 34 *You offspring of vipers! How can you speak good things when you are evil (wicked)? For out of the fullness (the overflow, the superabundance) of the heart the mouth speaks.* Vs. 35 *The good man from his inner good treasure flings forth good things, and the evil man out of his inner evil storehouse flings forth evil things.*

Vs. 36 *But I tell you, on the day of judgment men will have to give account for every idle (inoperative, nonworking) word they speak.* Vs. 37 *For by your words you will be justified and acquitted, and by your words you will be condemned and sentenced.*

In this world's system, we are raised to believe that the words we say do not have consequences, but they do. Jesus says that we must give an account for every negative, useless, silly word that we have spoken.

You are passing sentence on yourself with your mouth every day, whether you want to or not. "You nearly gave me a heart attack!" "We can't afford it!" "You are useless!" "You will never amount to anything!" "I am sick to death with you/this situation!" "I cannot do it!" "I am not good at that!" "I never get anything right!"

These are the devil's words. They are what he is saying to you. These are not the words that your Father speaks over you. Your Father says, "You are a blessing! You are blessed! You are loved! You are favored!"

FIFTY-THREE
DIFFERENT KINDS *of* PRAYER

Ephesians 6:18 *Praying always with all prayer and supplication in the Spirit, and watching thereunto with all perseverance and supplication for all saints.*

Even though prayer is discussed much, there is still little understanding concerning the subject. There are different kinds of prayer. As there are different kinds of sports, played by different rules, so it is with prayer—one "prayer" with different rules.

1 THE PRAYER OF CONSECRATION - IF IT BE THY WILL Luke 22:42 *Saying, Father, if thou be willing, remove this cup from me: nevertheless not my will, but thine, be done.* This is not a prayer to change things, but a prayer to consecrate your will to the will of God. "I will go where you want me to go; I will do what you want me to do; I will say what you want me to say; I will be what you want me to be."

2 THE PRAYER OF REPENTANCE - I John 1:9 *If we confess our sins, he is faithful and just to forgive us our sins, and to cleanse us from all unrighteousness.* This prayer should be prayed by the believer to keep himself in fellowship with God to avoid allowing "the little foxes to spoil the vines." (Song of Solomon 2:15)

3 THE PRAYER OF FORGIVENESS - Mark 11:25, 26 *And when ye stand praying, forgive, if ye have ought against any: that your Father also which is in heaven may forgive you your trespasses.*

But if ye do not forgive, neither will your Father which is in heaven forgive your trespasses. You must forgive others in order for God to forgive you.

4 THE PRAYER OF FAITH - (Mark 11:22-24) This is a prayer to change things — to get results to move mountains. Vs. 22 *And Jesus answering saith unto them, Have faith in God.* Vs. 23 *For verily I say unto you, That whosoever shall say unto this mountain, Be thou removed, and be thou cast into the sea: and shall not doubt in his heart, but shall believe that those things which he saith shall come to pass; he shall have whatsoever he saith.* Vs. 24 *Therefore I say unto you, What things soever ye desire, when ye pray, believe that ye receive them, and ye shall have them.* This is prayer based on the revealed will of God through His Word.

5 THE PRAYER OF COMMITTAL - Casting your cares upon the Lord **(I Peter 5:7)** *Casting all your care upon him; for he careth for you.* Some people are champion worriers; many times they are worried because they have nothing to worry about. (Taking every thought captive — II Corinthians 10:4, 5. Take no thought for tomorrow — Matthew 6:27)

6 THE PRAYER OF AGREEMENT - Binding and Loosing (Matthew 18:18-20) Vs. 18 *Verily I say unto you, Whatsoever ye shall bind on earth shall be bound in heaven: and whatsoever ye shall loose on earth shall be loosed in heaven.* Vs. 19 *Again I say unto you, That if two of you shall agree on earth as touching any thing that they shall ask, it shall be done for them of my Father which is in heaven.* Vs. 20 *For where two or three are gathered together in my name, there am I in the midst of them.* You can only bind what has been bound in heaven and you can only loose what has been loosed in heaven.

7 THE PRAYER OF WORSHIP (Acts 16:22-25) Vs. 22 *And the multitude rose up together against them: and the magistrates rent off their clothes and commanded to beat them.* Vs. 23 *And when* *they had laid many stripes upon them, they cast them into prison, charging the jailer to keep them safely:* Vs. 24 *Who, having received such a charge, thrust them into the inner prison, and made their feet fast in the stocks.* Vs. 25 *And at midnight Paul and Silas prayed, and sang praises unto God: and the prisoners heard them.* At midnight, in the darkest hour of your life, you can sing praises to God and God will deliver you.

8 UNITED PRAYER - (Acts 4:23-31) Vs. 23 *And being let go, they went to their own company, and reported all that the chief priests and elders had said unto them.* Vs. 24 *And when they heard that, they lifted up their voice to God with one accord, and said, Lord, thou art God, which hast made heaven, and earth, and the sea, and all that in them is:* Vs. 25 *Who by the mouth of thy servant David hast said, Why did the heathen rage, and the people imagine vain things?* Vs. 26 *The kings of the earth stood up, and the rulers were gathered together against the Lord, and against his Christ.*

Vs. 27 *For of a truth against thy holy child Jesus, whom thou hast anointed, both Herod, and Pontius Pilate, with the Gentiles, and the people of Israel, were gathered together,* Vs. 28 *For to do whatsover thy hand and thy counsel determined before to be done.* Vs. 29 *And now, Lord, behold their threatenings: and grant unto thy servants, that with all boldness they may speak thy word.* Vs. 30 *By stretching forth thine hand to heal; and that signs and wonders may be done by the name of thy holy child Jesus.* Vs. 31 *And when they had prayed, the place was shaken where they were assembled together; and they were filled with the Holy Ghost, and they spake the word of God with boldness.*

9. THE PRAYER OF INTERCESSION (I Timothy 2:1-5) Vs. 1 *I exhort therefore, that, first of all, supplications, prayers, intercessions, and giving of thanks, be made for all men;* Vs. 2 *For kings, and for all that are in authority; that we may lead a quiet and peaceable life in all godliness and honesty.* Vs. 3 *For this is good and acceptable in the sight of God our Saviour;* Vs. 4 *Who will have all men to be saved, and to come unto the knowledge of* *the truth. Vs. 5 For there is one God, and one mediator between God and men, the man Christ Jesus.*

10 PRAYING IN THE SPIRIT - (Jude 20) *But ye, beloved, building up yourselves on your most holy faith, praying in the Holy Ghost.*

FIFTY-FOUR
DELIGHT and DESIRE

Psalms 37:3-5 Vs. 3 *Trust in the LORD, and do good; so shalt thou dwell in the land, and verily thou shalt be fed.* Vs. 4 *Delight thyself also in the LORD; and he shall give thee the desires of thine heart.* Vs. 5 *Commit thy way unto the LORD; trust also in him; and he shall bring it to pass.*

When your delight is in the Lord, He will delight in giving you the desires of your heart. Not the desires of your *head* (or your flesh, or your carnal nature), but the desires of your *heart*.

The Greek word for "desire" in this passage means "request; desire; petition." When you are sold out to God and are in His will, He will take great delight in granting your requests, desires and petitions.

Proverbs 11:23 *The desire of the righteous is only good: but the expectation of the wicked is wrath.*

James 4:2, 3 *Ye lust, and have not: ye kill, and desire to have, and cannot obtain; ye fight and war, yet ye have not, because ye ask not. Ye ask, and receive not, because ye ask amiss, that ye may consume it upon your lusts.*

I John 5:14, 15 *And this is the confidence that we have in him, that, if we ask any thing according to his will, he heareth us: And if we know that he hear us, whatsoever we ask, we know that we have the petitions that we desired of him.*

It is not difficult to have your prayers answered and receive those things God has for you. The issue is whether or not you come to God with the right heart attitude. When our heart's desire is to please our Father in everything we do, He hears our prayers and requests, and if He hears, He answers. If we are covetous, mean or selfish, we are not praying according to His will and He does not hear and answer our requests.

Psalms 73:25 (Amp) *Whom have I in heaven but You? And I have no delight or desire on earth besides You.*

King David delighted in the Lord all the days of his life. Even when he made mistakes, he was humble and repentant before God. Because David delighted himself in God, God was delighted with David and blessed him and his seed abundantly.

Psalms 21:1-7 (Amp) Vs. 1 *The King [David] shall joy in Your strength, O Lord; and in Your salvation how greatly shall he rejoice!* Vs. 2 *You have given him his heart's desire and have not withheld the request of his lips. Selah.*

Vs. 3 *For You send blessings of good things to meet him; You set a crown of pure gold on his head.* Vs. 4 *He asked life of You, and You gave it to him-long life forever and evermore.* Vs. 5 *His glory is great because of Your aid; splendor and majesty You bestow upon him.*

Vs. 6 *For You make him to be blessed and a blessing forever; You make him exceedingly glad with the joy of Your presence.* Vs. 7 *For the king trusts, relies on, and is confident in the Lord, and through the mercy and steadfast love of the Most High he will never be moved.*

When you delight yourself in the Lord and trust, rely on and are confident in the Lord, He gives you your heart's desire and causes you to be blessed and a blessing forever.

FIFTY-FIVE
ALL-NIGHT PRAYER – PRAYING UNTO GOD

Luke 6:12 *And it came to pass in those days, that he went out into a mountain to pray, and continued all night in prayer to God.*

I Thessalonians 5:17 *Pray without ceasing.*

When our church had its first all-night prayer meeting, our people responded to the call to pray, and many prayed all night – twelve continuous hours of prayer before the Throne of God. We started with over 350 people and ended up with 120 people twelve hours later. Many confessed they had never spent that long a time in prayer.

I can remember being in all-night prayer meetings many times as a child and it had a great impact on my life.

Luke 2:36, 37 *And there was one Anna, a prophetess, the daughter of Phanuel, of the tribe of Aser: she was of a great age, and had lived with an husband seven years from her virginity; And she was a widow of about fourscore and four years, which departed not from the temple, but served God with fastings and prayers night and day.*

As a believer, there is a special place in prayer that you can find. Some have said that prayer changes things but prayer does not change things – people change things. As you pray, your heart changes. As your heart changes, your situation changes.

There is a need to teach on the subject of prayer because we have seen the confusion and the excesses of prayer as a result of incorrect teaching and practices. The Lord told me that we have to teach people to pray properly.

Luke 18:1-8 Vs. 1 *And He spake a parable unto them to this end, that men ought always to pray, and not to faint;* Vs. 2 *Saying, There was in a city a judge, which feared not God, neither regarded man:* Vs. 3 *And there was a widow in that city; and she came unto him, saying, Avenge me of mine adversary.*

Vs. 4 *And he would not for a while: but afterward he said within himself, Though I fear not God, nor regard man;* Vs. 5 *Yet because this widow troubleth me, I will avenge her, lest by her continual coming she weary me.* Vs. 6 *And the Lord said, Hear what the unjust judge saith.*

Vs. 7 *And shall not God avenge his own elect, which cry day and night unto him, though he bear long with them?* Vs. 8 *I tell you that he will avenge them speedily. Nevertheless when the Son of man cometh, shall he find faith on the earth?*

Jesus was talking about prevailing prayer, the kind of prayer that will bring victory in your life. It is not whining or nagging, but it is constancy. We need to pray regularly and consistently; it should become a lifestyle. Prayer is the world's highest trade and its skill takes a lifetime. Most people spend too much time talking about their problems instead of praying. Do not talk to everyone else about your problems – talk to the Father. He has the answer! There are also many people who teach on the subject of prayer but spend very little time in prayer themselves. If we preach it, we should do it.

Prayer is essential to a victorious Christian life. It dips you in the kerosene of the Spirit so that during your prayer time your heart will be set ablaze by the Holy Spirit.

FIFTY-SIX
BREAKING the MOLD of RELIGIOUS TRADITION

Luke 6:1-11 Vs. 1 *And it came to pass on the second sabbath after the first, that he went through the corn fields; and his disciples plucked the ears of corn, and did eat, rubbing them in their hands.* Vs. 2 *And certain of the Pharisees said unto them, Why do ye that which is not lawful to do on the sabbath days?*

Vs. 3 *And Jesus answering them said, Have ye not read so much as this, what David did, when himself was an hungered, and they which were with him;* Vs. 4 *How he went into the house of God, and did take and eat the showbread, and gave also to them that were with him; which it is not lawful to eat but for the priests alone?* Vs. 5 *And he said unto them, That the Son of man is Lord also of the sabbath.*

Vs. 6 *And it came to pass also on another sabbath, that he entered into the synagogue and taught: and there was a man whose right hand was withered.* Vs. 7 *And the scribes and Pharisees watched him, whether he would heal on the sabbath day; that they might find an accusation against him.* Vs. 8 *But he knew their thoughts, and said to the man which had the withered hand, Rise up, and stand forth in the midst. And he arose and stood forth.*

Vs. 9 *Then said Jesus unto them, I will ask you one thing; Is it lawful on the sabbath days to do good, or to do evil? to save life, or to destroy it?* Vs. 10 *And looking round about upon them all, he said unto the man, Stretch forth thy hand. And he did so: and his hand was restored whole as the other.* Vs. 11 *And they were filled with madness; and communed one with another what they might do to Jesus.*

Religion wants things done a certain way and does not care about people. Religion cares only about itself. It would rather keep people in bondage to the system, so that it can perpetuate itself. As long as you stay within the system of religion, you will be acceptable to everyone else, as well as the system. Religion thrives on bondage, bondage to a belief system, to certain ways of doing things, to a program of works rather than faith—without regard to the truth or the condition of a person's heart.

Mark 7:5-13 Vs. 5 *Then the Pharisees and scribes asked him, Why walk not thy disciples according to the tradition of the elders, but eat bread with unwashen hands?* Vs. 6 *He answered and said unto them, Well hath Esaias prophesied of you hypocrites, as it is written, This people honoureth me with their lips, but their heart is far from me.*

Vs. 7 *Howbeit in vain do they worship me, teaching for doctrines the commandments of men.* Vs. 8 *For laying aside the commandment of God, ye hold the tradition of men, as the washing of pots and cups: and many other such like things ye do.*

Vs. 9 *And he said unto them, Full well ye reject the commandment of God, that ye may keep your own tradition.* Vs. 10 *For Moses said, Honour thy father and thy mother; and, Whoso curseth father or mother, let him die the death:*

Vs. 11 *But ye say, If a man shall say to his father or mother, It is Corban, that is to say, a gift, by whatsoever thou mightest be profited by me; he shall be free.* Vs. 12 *And ye suffer him no more to do ought for his father or his mother;* Vs. 13 *Making the word of God of none effect through your tradition, which ye have delivered: and many such like things do ye.*

Jesus was the One Who came to break the mold of religious bondage. He made religious tradition (man's way) redundant when He said in **John 10:10:** *The thief cometh not, but for to steal, and to kill, and to destroy: I am come that they might have life, and that they might have it more abundantly.*

The thief—religion—steals, kills and destroys, but Jesus said, *"I am come that you might have life and that you might have it more abundantly."* Everywhere Jesus went, He broke the mold by breaking tradition. It was religion that finally nailed Him to the cross. The religious had to stop Him—He was setting too many people free. They felt they had to protect the system, and the only way to do that was to remove Him from the scene.

Jesus destroyed the *status quo* as He went about setting people free from religion and the bondage of man. If we want to break the mold, we have to get close to Him and walk in His ways, keep His commandments, and do His sayings.

FIFTY-SEVEN
FREE at LAST

John 8:30-36 Vs. 30 *As he spake these words, many believed on him.* Vs. 31 *Then said Jesus to those Jews which believed on him, If ye continue in my word, then are ye my disciples indeed.* Vs. 32 *And ye shall know the truth, and the truth shall make you free.*

Vs. 33 *They answered him, We be Abraham's seed, and were never in bondage to any man: how sayest thou, Ye shall be made free?* Vs. 34 *Jesus answered them, Verily, verily, I say unto you, Whosoever committeth sin is the servant of sin.*

Vs. 35 *And the servant abideth not in the house for ever: but the Son abideth ever.* Vs. 36 *If the Son therefore shall make you free, ye shall be free indeed.*

"Free at last, free at last! Thank God Almighty, we are free at last." Dr. Martin Luther King Jr. spoke these immortal words and they reflect the secret desires of every heart on earth. There is something inside every one of us that longs for freedom. Unfortunately, some people see freedom only when they leave this earth and others never see it at all — they simply go from the bondage of this world system to the ultimate bondage of hell.

The freedom that men long for in the natural is a reflection of the freedom they long to experience deep down in their heart. Freedom is often hard won. Usually, as in war, a few pay the price for the freedom of thousands of others. The fathers of this nation, and others down through the years, gave up their lands, their fortunes, and their lives for freedom that they considered worthy of the sacrifice. Not all of them saw the fruit of their labors, but they were aware from the start that their fruit would be enjoyed by others, yet unborn. Their sacrifice would bless those who would not have to pay the ultimate price.

Everyone who has stood up for something that they believed in, for a freedom they felt they deserved, has paid a price. Sometimes those who come generations afterward do not appreciate the sacrifice, even as they enjoy the freedom purchased by another. There is a freedom that was bought at great cost. It took God Himself, born in human form, mocked, scourged and brutally crucified, to buy us the ultimate freedom—freedom from sin and death and the devil. Freedom to be called God's own and freedom to serve Him fully.

Mark 7:6, 7 & 13 Vs. 6 *He answered and said unto them, Well hath Esaias prophesied of you hypocrites, as it is written, This people honoureth me with their lips, but their heart is far from me.* Vs. 7 *Howbeit in vain do they worship me, teaching for doctrines the commandments of men.* Vs. 13 *Making the word of God of none effect through your tradition, which ye have delivered: and many such like things do ye.*

Some people equate bondage with serving God, and freedom with sin. That is because even though the devil cannot stop anyone from serving God, he tries to get them into the bondage of religious tradition. When people are bound by tradition, the Word of God becomes ineffective in their lives. People can be deeply religious, then die and go to the bondage of hell anyway, because they tried to reach God their way—not His way. Other people believe they are free when they do things their way. They subscribe to the lie "I did it my way!" The devil gets them to yield to sin, and the more they sin, the more they become bound by sin. When they are bound by sin, the devil maintains control over them.

Romans 6:16 (Amp) *Do you not know that if you continually surrender yourselves to anyone to do his will, you are the slaves of him whom you obey, whether that be to sin, which leads to death, or to obedience which leads to righteousness (right doing and right standing with God)?*

God has given us freedom of choice—we can choose to serve Him or not. The world believes that true freedom is freedom to yield to their flesh and carnal nature, but the more you yield to sin and the flesh, the more you become enslaved by them. The more you yield to God, the more freedom you have. It does not matter what your physical state is, whether you are bound or free, Jesus is the ultimate freedom. To have His freedom in your heart and life is something that no devil, no man, no jail, and no death can control or bind up. We are free in Jesus as we obey His Word. To be free in Jesus is to be free indeed!

THE WORD *of* GOD IS TRUE *and* THE TRUTH *will* MAKE YOU FREE!

FIFTY-EIGHT
NO MORE JUDGMENT

John 3:14-21 (Amp) Vs. 14 *And just as Moses lifted up the serpent in the desert [on a pole], so must [so it is necessary that] the Son of Man be lifted up [on the cross],* Vs. 15 *In order that everyone who believes in Him [who cleaves to Him, trusts Him, and relies on Him] may not perish, but have eternal life and [actually] live forever!*

Vs. 16 *For God so greatly loved and dearly prized the world that He [even] gave up His only begotten (unique) Son, so that whoever believes in (trusts in, clings to, relies on) Him shall not perish (come to destruction, be lost) but have eternal (everlasting) life.* Vs. 17 *For God did not send the Son into the world in order to judge (to reject, to condemn, to pass sentence on) the world, but that the world might find salvation and be made safe and sound through Him.*

Vs. 18 *He who believes in Him [who clings to, trusts in, relies on Him] is not judged [he who trusts in Him never comes up for judgment; for him there is no rejection, no condemnation-he incurs no damnation]; but he who does not believe (cleave to, rely on, trust in Him) is judged already [he has already been convicted and has already received his sentence] because he has not believed in and trusted in the name of the only begotten Son of God. [He is condemned for refusing to let his trust rest in Christ's name.]*

Vs. 19 *The [basis of the] judgment (indictment, the test by which men are judged, the ground for the sentence) lies in this: the Light has come into the world, and people have loved the darkness rather than and more than the Light, for their works (deeds) were evil.*

Vs. 20 *For every wrongdoer hates (loathes, detests) the Light, and will not come out into the Light but shrinks from it, lest his works (his deeds, his activities, his conduct) be exposed and reproved.*

Vs. 21 *But he who practices truth [who does what is right] comes out into the Light; so that his works may be plainly shown to be what they are-wrought with God [divinely prompted, done with God's help, in dependence upon Him].*

The gospel is a simple message, but it is far too simple for some people, so they try to make it complicated. They labor under the mistaken belief that it cannot possibly be so easy, so they try to make it harder. They create rules and regulations for people to keep in order to earn God's favor.

The bottom line of the gospel is this: the world is under a sentence of judgment already and Jesus came to lift that sentence. The devil would like us to believe that God loves sending people to hell and that He has made it very hard to get into heaven. The lie is that God is not a "fun guy" but the devil is a fun guy. People declare that they would rather go to hell and party with the devil than be in a boring, restrictive heaven. Or they believe there is no hell and no judgment, that we all go to heaven because of our good works, and any religion is right because we all worship the same God.

Well, there is only one true God – I AM THAT I AM. He has testified through the ages to His own existence and His plan for man. If we do not serve or worship Him the way He tells us to – not the way mere men tell us to – then we are not worshipping Him at all. The truth is that this earth was once filled with His presence and it was a paradise. The liar (the devil) deceived man and caused him to sin, to lose the presence of God, and without God's divine intervention, we were all doomed to eternal hell. Jesus came to save us from the destiny for which we were headed. He came to change our destiny, to give us the opportunity to come back into the presence of God for all eternity.

Jesus did not come to judge us—because we were already judged. He came to remove the sentence of judgment and allow us to live as free men. If men die and go to hell, it is because they have chosen their own sentence, not because God has willed it for them. God's will for us is that none should perish, but that all should come to repentance (II Peter 3:9).

FIFTY-NINE
FAITH – *the* TITLE DEED

Hebrews 11:1-3 Vs. 1 *Now faith is the substance of things hoped for, the evidence of things not seen.* **Vs. 2** *For by it the elders obtained a good report.* **Vs. 3** *Through faith we understand that the worlds were framed by the word of God, so that things which are seen were not made of things which do appear.*

Hebrews 11: 1-3 (Amp) Vs. 1 *Now faith is the assurance (the confirmation, the title deed) of the things [we] hope for, being the proof of things [we] do not see and the conviction of their reality [faith perceiving as real fact what is not revealed to the senses].*

Vs. 2 *For by [faith-trust and holy fervor born of faith] the men of old had divine testimony borne to them and obtained a good report.* Vs. 3 *By faith we understand that the worlds [during the successive ages] were framed (fashioned, put in order, and equipped for their intended purpose) by the word of God, so that what we see was not made out of things which are visible.*

When Jesus died on the cross, He purchased our redemption from sin, sickness, poverty and death. In the Bible, the Greek word for salvation also means healing, deliverance, and preservation. By His stripes we were healed (I Peter 2:24) and He was made poor so that we could be rich (II Corinthians 8:9).

God has promised us many good things in His Word. He promises us good things for our spirit, soul and body, but they do not come to us just because we are Christians or because we live a good life. It is good to be a Christian and to be a good person, but God's promises become ours when we believe them and take them for ourselves. It takes a little faith on our part—not just hoping or wishing or complaining. Some people think that God owes them something, but God owes us nothing. He has made promises and He is waiting for us to claim them with our faith.

If we do not use our faith to appropriate the promises of God, we are like the person who received notification that he had won a $10,000 prize and all he had to do was claim it—but he never bothered to get in the car to fetch it. It was his all along, but he could not receive the benefit of it until he fetched it and brought it home.

Faith is the substance, the assurance, the confirmation, and the title deed of the things we hope for. Just hoping will not bring the promises to fulfillment—we must apply faith to our hope. By the same token, we cannot have faith without first having hope. Faith is like a title deed. It is as if you inherited a piece of land and at the reading of the will you are given the title deed. You may never have stood on your property or even seen it, but if you have the title deed in your possession, you know it is your land. It is a sure thing! God's word is a sure thing. When you use your faith to appropriate God's promises, your faith is like the title deed. You cannot see it, feel it, hear it, touch it or taste it, but you know that it is yours and no one can tell you otherwise.

Faith is the evidence and proof of the things we do not see, and the conviction of their reality. Faith perceives as real fact what is not revealed to the senses. You cannot see the promise of God, but you know it is real and it is yours. Faith can see what your eyes cannot see. Faith looks into the realm where God lives and grabs hold of the promise. Faith brings the promise to you from the supernatural realm into the natural realm.

This entire world was created by the world we cannot see. God created the universe with His faith, and we bring what we need from God to us by our faith. Nothing is impossible to him who believes (Mark 9:23). Faith is simply this: believing that God will do what He said He would do. Faith is simply trusting God, believing His Word, acting like all of it is true. Children find it easier to believe God because they have not been disappointed yet.

We are afraid to trust, because people let us down and lie to us, but God cannot lie and He will not disappoint us (Numbers 23:19). You can trust Him to always back up His Word as you stand in faith with no doubts. If God said it, you can believe it and it can be yours.

SIXTY
BELIEVING GOD *for* BIG THINGS

Ephesians 3:20 *Now unto him that is able to do exceeding abundantly above all that we ask or think, according to the power that worketh in us.*

Many times we limit God because of our small thinking. God does not think like a man or operate like a man. Man's ways are limited, but God's ways are unlimited.

Isaiah 55:8-10 Vs. 8 *For my thoughts are not your thoughts, neither are your ways my ways, saith the Lord.* Vs. 9 *For as the heavens are higher than the earth, so are my ways higher than your ways, and my thoughts than your thoughts.*

Vs. 10 *For as the rain cometh down, and the snow from heaven, and returneth not thither, but watereth the earth, and maketh it bring forth and bud, that it may give seed to the sower, and bread to the eater . . .*

God is letting us know that His thinking and our thinking are worlds apart. We need to change our way of thinking to think the thoughts of God. Many of God's people are limited by their carnal thinking. They see their limitations and they put God in the same box. God is unlimited in His ability — where man's limitation ends, God's ability begins.

Job, after all his disaster, presumptuously rambled on and on with his friends, until God finally revealed Himself to him and straightened him out. Then Job said, "I have heard of thee by the hearing of the ear: but now mine eye seeth thee." (Job 42:5)

It is one thing to hear about Him—it is another thing to actually *know* Him. Many people have heard of Him, but they do not really know Him. You need to see Him as He really is—an awesome God. He is the One Who created the heavens and the earth and formed them by the words of His mouth.

Hebrews 11:3 *Through faith we understand that the worlds were framed by the word of God, so that things which are seen were not made of things which do appear.*

Genesis 1:1-3 *In the beginning God created the heaven and the earth. And the earth was without form, and void; and darkness was upon the face of the deep. And the Spirit of God moved upon the face of the waters. And God said, Let there be light: and there was light.*

This is the God that you and I serve. There are no limitations with Him; what He speaks—happens.

Psalms 8:1-9 Vs. 1 *O Lord our Lord, how excellent is thy name in all the earth! who hast set thy glory above the heavens.* Vs. 2 *Out of the mouth of babes and sucklings hast thou ordained strength because of thine enemies, that thou mightest still the enemy and the avenger.*

Vs. 3 *When I consider thy heavens, the work of thy fingers, the moon and the stars, which thou hast ordained;* Vs. 4 *What is man, that thou art mindful of him? and the son of man, that thou visitest him?* Vs. 5 *For thou hast made him a little lower than the angels, and hast crowned him with glory and honour.*

Vs. 6 *Thou madest him to have dominion over the works of thy hands; thou hast put all things under his feet:* Vs. 7 *All sheep and oxen, yea, and the beasts of the field;* Vs. 8 *The fowl of the air, and the fish of the sea, and whatsoever passeth through the paths of the seas.* Vs. 9 *O Lord our Lord, how excellent is thy name in all the earth!*

HE IS OMNIPRESENT — which means He is everywhere.
HE IS OMNIPOTENT — which means He is all-powerful.
HE IS OMNISCIENT — which means He knows everything.

Nothing is impossible with God — there are no limitations with Him. With His finger He created the world and with His arm, He saved and redeemed men. That shows you how much effort He had to use — not much. He is an awesome God — believe Him for big things — trust Him for great things today!

SIXTY-ONE
DO NOT BE *the* JUDGE

John 3:17 (Amp) *For God did not send the Son into the world in order to judge (to reject to condemn, to pass sentence on) the world, but that the world might find salvation and be made safe and sound through Him.*

Jesus was sent by the Father — not to judge and condemn the world, but to save the world from sin and judgment. As His representatives here on earth, we are not better than He is and we have neither a right nor a mandate to stand in judgment of a sinner or a saint. We are to speak the truth in love, but we are not called to judge or criticize.

Matthew 7:1-5 (Amp) Vs. 1 *Do not judge or criticize and condemn others, so that you may not be judged and criticized and condemned yourselves.* Vs. 2 *For just as you judge and criticize and condemn others, you will be judged and criticized and condemned, and in accordance with the measure you [use to] deal out to others, it will be dealt out again to you.*

Vs. 3 *Why do you stare from without at the very small particle that is in your brother's eye, but do not become aware of and consider the beam of timber that is in your own eye?* Vs. 4 *Or how can you say to your brother, let me get the tiny particle out of your eye, when there is a beam of timber in your own eye?* Vs. 5 *You hypocrite, first get the beam of timber out of your own eye, and then you will see clearly to take the tiny particle out of your brother's eye.*

God's laws of sowing and reaping work all the time, in everything you do and say — whether good or bad. We want the good things we do to come back to bless us, but sometimes we forget that the bad things we do and say also come back to us. If we remember that we are judged by the same standards wherewith we judge others, we will most likely not judge quite as critically as we sometimes do. Most times, we judge ourselves according to our MOTIVES, but we judge others according to their ACTIONS. We may do something wrong, but we meant well, so we judge ourselves lightly, if at all. If another person does something we do not like, we feel free to judge them on their actions without considering their motivation.

John 8:15, 16 (Amp) Vs. 15 *You [set yourselves up to] judge according to the flesh (by what you see). [You condemn by external human standards.] I do not [set Myself up to] judge or condemn or sentence anyone.* Vs. 16 *Yet even if I do judge, My judgment is true [My decision is right]; for I am not alone [in making it], but [there are two of Us] I and the Father, Who sent Me.*

Jesus does not judge us by human standards, according to the flesh (outward appearance). Jesus judges the heart of man and knows what lies therein. We do not know men's hearts (unless God shows us), so it is better for us to withhold our judgment and do what I Corinthians 13:7 says: believe the best (not the worst) of every person. Many times we are much more apt to believe something bad — rather than something good — about another person.

It seems as if people with the most faults themselves are the ones who always notice the faults in others. The most critical people usually are unhappy with themselves. They think they can cover their faults by pointing out everyone else's. In the Church, usually people who criticize the pastor and fellow Christians are the ones who are under conviction of the Holy Spirit because of a fault or sin in their own life. They will not change nor admit that they are wrong, so in order to justify themselves, they attack and find fault with others who are living right.

Romans 14:12, 13 (Amp) Vs. 12 *And so each of us shall give an account of himself [give an answer in reference to judgment] to God.* Vs. 13 *Then let us no more criticize and blame and pass judgment on one another, but rather decide and endeavor never to put a stumbling block or an obstacle or a hindrance in the way of a brother.*

We need to learn to focus on ourselves, clean up our act, and leave our brothers and sisters in God's hands. There is a very good reason why God tells us to pray for even our enemies — so that we can keep our hearts free and pure. When we are praying for someone, it is hard to also be criticizing him or her or be angry with them. Remember, we may have a REASON to judge another person, but we do not have the RIGHT.

SIXTY-TWO
BE YOUR *own* JUDGE

I Corinthians 11:31, 32 (Amp) Vs. 31 *For if we searchingly examined ourselves [detecting our short-comings and recognizing our own condition], we should not be judged and penalty decreed [by the divine judgment].* Vs. 32 *But when we [fall short and] are judged by the Lord, we are disciplined and chastened, so that we may not [finally] be condemned [to eternal punishment along] with the world.*

It is always better for us to check our own heart condition and judge ourselves than to wait and be judged by God. Jesus did not come to judge the world but to save it, since it was already under a sentence of judgment (John 3:17 and 18).

When we receive Jesus as Lord and Savior, the sentence is removed and eternal life becomes our inheritance. God gives us the right to choose to serve Him and have the judgment removed. It is important for us to realize that we are to judge our own hearts and lives and act accordingly to conform to God's image.

The Holy Spirit is here to show us the way, to teach us and rebuke us, if necessary. The Word of God is our standard and our guide.

II Timothy 3:16 and 17 (Amp) Vs. 16 *Every Scripture is God-breathed (given by His inspiration) and profitable for instruction, for reproof and conviction of sin, for correction of error and discipline in obedience, [and] for training in righteousness (in* *holy living, in conformity to God's will in thought, purpose, and action),* Vs. 17 *So that the man of God may be complete and proficient, well fitted and thoroughly equipped for every good work.*

Our Father will correct, discipline and train us through His Word and we must be teachable and open to His instruction if we want to be blessed in every area of our lives.

Proverbs 3:11-13 Vs. 11 *My son, despise not the chastening of the Lord; neither be weary of his correction:* Vs. 12 *For whom the Lord loveth he correcteth; even as a father the son in whom he delighteth.* Vs. 13 *Happy is the man that findeth wisdom, and the man that getteth understanding.*

Some people believe that God disciplines us with sickness and suffering, but this belief is not consistent with the whole of the scriptures. God corrects us by the Spirit and the Word. Now if through disobedience we remove ourselves from His protection and get out in the enemy's territory, we may suffer all kinds of calamity — but it does not originate with God.

James 1:13-17 (Amp) Vs. 13 *Let no one say when he is tempted, I am tempted from God: for God is incapable of being tempted by [what is] evil and He Himself tempts no one.* Vs. 14 *But every person is tempted when he is drawn away, enticed and baited by his own evil desire (lust, passions).*

Vs. 15 *Then the evil desire, when it has conceived, gives birth to sin, and sin, when it is fully matured, brings forth death.* Vs. 16 *Do not be misled, my beloved brethren.*

Vs. 17 *Every good gift and every perfect (free, large, full) gift is from above; it comes down from the Father of all [that gives] light, in [the shining of] Whom there can be no variation [rising or setting] or shadow cast by His turning [as in an eclipse].*

Every man's heart is his own responsibility. We are not responsible for another man's heart and they are not responsible for ours. If we keep tabs on our own situation and make the necessary judgments and adjustments, we cannot be judged by man and we will not be judged (in a bad way) by God.

I John 4:17 *Herein is our love made perfect, that we may have boldness in the day of judgment: because as he is, so are we in this world.*

If we do what pleases God, and allow His Spirit to change us and His love to dwell in our hearts, we do not need to be afraid to stand before Him on the day of judgment.

SIXTY-THREE
GOD'S WORD *is* TRUE *and* SURE

I Kings 8:56 *Blessed be the Lord, that hath given rest unto his people Israel, according to all that he promised: there hath not failed one word of all his good promise, which he promised by the hand of Moses his servant.*

God's Word is true and sure. He never fails to do what He promised — you can trust His Word absolutely. We all make promises, but not one of us has ever kept 100 percent of the promises we have made in our lives. How wonderful that God has kept *every promise* He has ever made. Men have failed God, but God has never failed men. God is full of righteousness and justice — He never lies and His Word never lies.

Psalm 33:4-9 Vs. 4 *For the word of the Lord is right; and all his works are done in truth.* Vs. 5 *He loveth righteousness and judgment: the earth is full of the goodness of the Lord.* Vs. 6 *By the word of the Lord were the heavens made; and all the host of them by the breath of his mouth.*

Vs. 7 *He gathereth the waters of the sea together as an heap: he layeth up the depth in storehouses.* Vs. 8 *Let all the earth fear the Lord: let all the inhabitants of the world stand in awe of him.* Vs. 9 *For he spake, and it was done; he commanded, and it stood fast.*

God created the world by and with His words. He spoke and it happened exactly as He spoke it. If He created the whole universe with His words, then surely anything else He says and anything He promises will also come to pass. His Word is *true, righteous* and *just.* If we really believed that, we would conduct our lives very differently from the way we do. If we were founded and established on the truth of God's Word, we would not lack nor fail.

Psalm 107:19-21 Vs. 19 *Then they cry unto the Lord in their trouble, and he saveth them out of their distresses.* Vs. 20 *He sent his word, and healed them, and delivered them from their destructions.* Vs. 21 *Oh that men would praise the Lord for his goodness, and for his wonderful works to the children of men!*

God gave His Word to heal us and deliver us from sin and destruction. God's Word is the source of our deliverance! God's Word is the blueprint for our lives. He made us; He knows what we need. He knows how we tick and He knows what is good for us. Our lives should be ordered according to His Word. However, we will not order our lives in the way God desires until we *know* His Word and believe it to be absolutely true and sure.

We must know that we can trust His Word in our lives. God's Word will never fail us; it will never let us down. We can praise God for His Word, because it is true whether we see it or not. As we praise Him and as we believe His Word, we will see it come to pass in our lives.

Psalm 138:2 *I will worship toward thy holy temple, and praise thy name for thy lovingkindness and for thy truth: for thou hast magnified thy word above all thy name.*

God's Word is full of integrity—He holds His own Word in high regard. There is a saying, "You are only as good as your word." This means that your worth depends on your integrity. God is as good as His Word!

Numbers 23:19 *God is not a man, that he should lie; neither the son of man, that he should repent: hath he said, and shall he not do it? Or hath he spoken, and shall he not make it good?*

There are some things God cannot do. One of them is that He cannot lie. If He speaks it, He will do it. If He promises it, He will make sure that it comes to pass. When you understand that God's Word is absolutely true, you can begin to receive it exactly as it is written and you can receive it as *true* for *you*.

SIXTY-FOUR
TRAIN *your* CHILD WHILE THERE *is* HOPE

Proverbs 23:24 *The father of the righteous shall greatly rejoice: and he that begetteth a wise child shall have joy of him.*

Proverbs 10: 1 *The proverbs of Solomon. A wise son maketh a glad father: but a foolish son is the heaviness of his mother.*

Raising wise children and sending them into the world to succeed and prosper is a great accomplishment. A foolish child who makes a shipwreck of his life brings great pain and heartache, but a wise child brings great joy and satisfaction. A wise, successful child is something every normal parent wants, but it is not something that happens all by itself — we are the primary influences in helping shape our children in either a positive or a negative way.

Proverbs 19:18 *Chasten thy son while there is hope, and let not thy soul spare for his crying.* (King James Version)

Discipline your son, for in that there is hope; do not be a willing party to his death. (New International Version)

Chasten thy son, seeing there is hope; and set not thy heart on his destruction. (American Standard Version)

The Hebrew word for "chasten" also mean to chastise, correct, instruct, punish, reform, reprove, and teach. It is our primary responsibility, as parents, to teach, instruct, and correct our own children. This process of discipline is something that should begin very early in a child's life, while there is still hope. There is still hope when a child is very young. Children are not born a completely blank slate. They are born with definite personalities and we, as parents, can bring out the best or the worst in those personalities by our right training, wrong training, or lack of training. The earlier we begin with good training, the better our results will be.

Proverbs 29:17 *Correct thy son, and he shall give thee rest; yea, he shall give delight unto thy soul.*

Discipline your son and he will give you peace; he will bring delight to your soul. (NIV)

If we correct and discipline our children and raise them in God's ways from an early age, in their older years we will experience a peacefulness and delightfulness of a godly, wise child. If we do not properly correct and discipline our children according to the Word of God, we may experience the heartbreak and anguish of a foolish child, one who proceeds to ruin his own life and that of others.

As parents, the responsibility of raising our children is placed squarely upon our shoulders. With God's help, and our faith in Him and His Word, we can do it if we begin the training process early in their lives!

SIXTY-FIVE
OUR DELIVERER *has* COME

Isaiah 53:1-12 (Amp) Vs. 1 *Who has believed (trusted in, relied upon, and clung to) our message [of that which was revealed to us]? And to whom has the arm of the Lord been disclosed?* Vs. 2 *For [the Servant of God] grew up before Him like a tender plant, and like a root out of dry ground; He has no form or comeliness [royal, kingly pomp], that we should look at Him, and no beauty that we should desire Him.*

Vs. 3 *He was despised and rejected and forsaken by men, a Man of sorrows and pains, and acquainted with grief and sickness; and like One from Whom men hide their faces He was despised, and we did not appreciate His worth or have any esteem for Him.* Vs. 4 *Surely he has borne our griefs (sicknesses, weaknesses and distresses) and carried our sorrows and pains [of punishment], yet we [ignorantly] considered Him stricken, smitten, and afflicted by God [as if with leprosy].*

Vs. 5 *But He was wounded for our transgressions, He was bruised for our guilt and iniquities; the chastisement [needful to obtain] peace and well-being for us was upon Him, and with the stripes [that wounded] Him we are healed and made whole.* Vs. 6 *All we like sheep have gone astray, we have turned every one to his own way; and the Lord has made to light upon Him the guilt and iniquity of us all.*

Vs. 7 *He was oppressed, [yet when] He was afflicted, He was submissive and opened not his mouth; like a lamb that is led to the slaughter, and as a sheep before her shearers is dumb, so He opened not His mouth.* Vs. 8 *By oppression and judgment He was taken away; and as for His generation, who among them considered that He was cut off out of the land of the living [stricken to His death] for the transgression of my people, to whom the stroke was due?*

Vs. 9 *And they assigned Him a grave with the wicked, and with a rich man in His death, although He had done no violence, neither was any deceit in His mouth.* Vs. 10 *Yet it was the will of the Lord to bruise Him; He has put Him to grief and made Him sick. When You and He make His life an offering for sin [and He has risen from the dead, in time to come], He shall see His [spiritual] offspring, He shall prolong His days, and the will and pleasure of the Lord shall prosper in His hand.*

Vs. 11 *He shall see [the fruit] of the travail of His soul, and be satisfied; by His knowledge of Himself [which He possesses and imparts to others] shall My [uncompromisingly] righteous One, My Servant, justify many and make many righteous (upright and in right standing with God), for He shall bear their iniquities and their guilt [with the consequences, says the Lord].*

Vs. 12 *Therefore will I divide Him a portion with the great [kings and rulers], and He shall divide the spoil with the mighty, because He poured out His life unto death, and [He let Himself] be regarded as a criminal and be numbered with the transgressors; yet He bore [and took away] the sin of many and made intercession for the transgressors (the rebellious).*

This entire passage of Isaiah is a prophecy given generations before the death, burial and resurrection of our Lord and Savior, Jesus Christ, yet it describes the whole event in perfect detail. Jesus fulfilled every part of this prophecy and it is as true and real for us as it was for the first of His "spiritual offspring" (verse 10) — the early church. We are our Father God's spiritual offspring and we do not esteem Jesus' sacrifice lightly. He paid no small price to deliver us from sickness and sin—iniquity, grief and torment. If we refuse to accept the deliverance that Jesus bought and paid for, then we despise His great sacrifice. With great humility, let us gladly receive everything Jesus paid for, and honor His gift by walking in the freedom He purchased for us.

SIXTY-SIX
A SPIRIT *of* WISDOM *and* REVELATION

Ephesians 1:15-23 (New American Standard) Vs. 15 *For this reason I too, having heard of the faith in the Lord Jesus which exists among you, and your love for all the saints,*

Vs. 16 *Do not cease giving thanks for you, while making mention of you in my prayers;* Vs. 17 *That the God of our Lord Jesus Christ, the Father of glory, may give to you a spirit of wisdom and of revelation in the knowledge of Him.* Vs. 18 *I pray that the eyes of your heart may be enlightened, so that you may know what is the hope of His calling, what are the riches of the glory of His inheritance in the saints,*

Vs. 19 *And what is the surpassing greatness of His power toward us who believe. These are in accordance with the working of the strength of His might* Vs. 20 *Which He brought about in Christ, when He raised Him from the dead, and seated Him at His right hand in the heavenly places,*

Vs. 21 *Far above all rule and authority and power and dominion, and every name that is named, not only in this age, but also in the one to come.* Vs. 22 *And He put all things in subjection under His feet, and gave Him as head over all things to the church,* Vs. 23 *Which is His body, the fulness of Him who fills all in all.*

Ephesians 3:14-21 (NAS) Vs. 14 *For this reason, I bow my knees before the Father,* Vs. 15 *From whom every family in heaven and on earth derives its name,* Vs. 16 *That He would grant you,* *according to the riches of His glory, to be strengthened with power through His Spirit in the inner man;*

Vs. 17 *So that Christ may dwell in your hearts through faith; and that you, being rooted and grounded in love,* Vs. 18 *May be able to comprehend with all the saints what is the breadth and length and height and depth,* Vs. 19 *And to know the love of Christ which surpasses knowledge, that you may be filled up to all the fulness of God.*

Vs. 20 *Now to Him who is able to do exceeding abundantly beyond all that we ask or think, according to the power that works within us,* Vs. 21 *To Him be the glory in the church and in Christ Jesus to all generations forever and ever. Amen.*

I believe that each of us wants to know God better and we all want a deeper understanding of the things of God. Some people run into trouble because they want a deeper revelation—so deep that God does not even know what they are talking about! Or they want a "new" revelation—so new that God has not even heard of it! There is no "new" revelation. God is the same yesterday, today and forever. The revelation is the same—it is just sitting there, waiting to be uncovered by the sincere, hungry believer. It is "new" because it is new to you! Things are always new the first time you hear them.

I believe these two prayers in Ephesians, prayed by Paul, are also the prayers of Jesus for you. God is not withholding Himself from us; we are the ones who do not make the effort to come into His presence to receive from Him. Sometimes we make the effort to know Him better, but because we come with preconceived ideas, we are not open to hear the truth.

We should be hungry for the truth, not just for "new" revelation. Pray these prayers sincerely, in faith, out loud over yourself (change the "you" to "me") every day for a month and see what happens! Also, do not forget to read your Bible daily with a humble (teachable) spirit. I believe you will begin to grow incredibly in the things of God.

SIXTY-SEVEN
PARTNERSHIP

I Corinthians 3:7-9 Vs. 7 *So then neither is he that planteth any thing, neither he that watereth; but God that giveth the increase. Vs. 8 Now he that planteth and he that watereth are one: and every man shall receive his own reward according to his own labour. Vs. 9 For we are labourers together with God: ye are God's husbandry, ye are God's building.*

II Corinthians 6:1 *We then, as workers together with him, beseech you also that ye receive not the grace of God in vain.*

Philippians 4:14-19 Vs. 14 *Notwithstanding ye have well done, that ye did communicate with my affliction. Vs. 15 Now ye Philippians know also, that in the beginning of the gospel, when I departed from Macedonia, no church communicated with me as concerning giving and receiving, but ye only.*

Vs. 16 *For even in Thessalonica ye sent once and again unto my necessity. Vs. 17 Not because I desire a gift: but I desire fruit that may abound to your account. Vs. 18 But I have all, and abound: I am full, having received of Epaphroditus the things which were sent from you, an odour of a sweet smell, a sacrifice acceptable, well-pleasing to God. Vs. 19 But my God shall supply all your need according to his riches in glory by Christ Jesus.*

The Word of God makes it clear that partnership with a ministry is scriptural, and this is not a new thing. God has ordained that people join with ministries and hold up their hands. We are laborers together with the Lord. The anointing that is on this ministry comes into your life the moment you partner with this ministry. Because you become covenanted or joined together with us in helping spread revival around the world, you share in the same reward that the ministry receives. Every soul saved comes to your account. God notices every little thing you do, and He is not unrighteous to forget your labor of love.

Philippians 4:17 (Amp) *Not that I seek or am eager for [your] gift, but I do seek and am eager for the fruit which increases to your credit [the harvest of blessing that is accumulating to your account].*

Matthew 6:19-21 Vs. 19 *Lay not up for yourselves treasures upon earth, where moth and rust doth corrupt, and where thieves break through and steal:* Vs. 20 *But lay up for yourselves treasures in heaven, where neither moth nor rust doth corrupt, and where thieves do not break through nor steal:* Vs. 21 *For where your treasure is, there will your heart be also.*

Jesus said that where your treasure is, your heart will be. I am convinced that when many get to heaven, they will be surprised to see all that they laid up there because of their generosity down here on earth. On the other hand, many will be disappointed because they did not do more for the Kingdom of God.

Adonica and I would like to thank our partners from all over America who join us in praying for this ministry and support us financially. We appreciate your commitment to the Lord and to us. Without you, we would not be able to see the fulfillment of our dream of seeing America shaken by revival. We love you, our friends and partners!